EMBATTLED
PROJECTS

Biblical Secrets and Practical Advice
for Turning Around Your Failing Projects

GWYN MYERS PhD

WESTBOW
PRESS®
A DIVISION OF THOMAS NELSON
& ZONDERVAN

WestBow Press books may be ordered through booksellers or by contacting:

WestBow Press
A Division of Thomas Nelson & Zondervan
1663 Liberty Drive
Bloomington, IN 47403
www.westbowpress.com
844-714-3454

ISBN: 978-1-6642-7273-6 (sc)
ISBN: 978-1-6642-7274-3 (hc)
ISBN: 978-1-6642-7275-0 (e)

Library of Congress Control Number: 2022913113

Print information available on the last page.

WestBow Press rev. date: 07/29/2022

CONTENTS

GUARANTEED TO FAIL

"What do you think about the new project management office?" asked my boss about the newly established PMO, which would also report to him.

"It'll fail," I told him bluntly.

He was stunned by my response and asked why I, a person who rarely saw the glass anything but half-full, would say that.

"Because I know it will!" I said.

That answer was the result of many years of frustrating experience with all forms of project management. Projects and any associated management structure such as a project management office notoriously fail an astoundingly high percentage of the time. You've picked up this book, so you undoubtedly know this as well.

My prediction proved true. After only three months, this particular PMO failed setting the record in my experience. In those years of experience, I have found that PMOs primarily failed for one basic reason: they require that all projects throughout an entire company be managed by one separate functional unit, the PMO. Many other organization units or departments want to manage their own projects and of course the corresponding budgets. If the total company is not tightly structured with enforceable discipline, the projects will not be turned over and the PMO will fail.

Unfortunately, with or without a PMO, a high percentage of projects fail. Executives are reluctant to admit failure, so once they realize a project isn't working, they will instead stop it in its tracks and call it phase 1. They will publish a list of objectives accomplished and state that they will consider any other goals for future phases or projects. Then they will declare victory and move on or will just let it drift into the night, the project fading from memory as time passes.

No wonder project management is rarely successful. In this book, I bring together many issues that never seem to be resolved to the satisfaction of anyone in the business world and for the most part in the lives of individuals, yet all these issues must be solved for a project to be successful. Consider some of these examples.

Differing opinions. Senior executives discuss their open-door policy and invite you to express your opinions on issues large and small. If yours is a contrary opinion, you soon learn not to share that opinion until your resume is updated and on the street.

Performance reviews. Staff performance reviews have become so problematic that the current trend is to abolish them.

Communication. Many in the workplace now define a high form of communication as text messages between people sitting in the same office.

Decision Making. Which way are we going with that decision? Maybe we should invite other offices to weigh in on it. Let's get additional input. How about revisiting this after the first of the year? And on and on with no decision being made.

My frustration over these types of issues and their difficult resolutions did not come as an overnight *Ah ha!* after a short period of observation or involvement. No. It came after more than thirty years of serving in management positions—from working as a chief information officer, chief restructuring officer, and consultant on general assessment and strategic direction and as a turnaround executive for organizations, departments, locations, and projects. I have even studied these issues all the way to a PhD in management from Claremont Graduate University. My management consulting work included projects with companies large and small, public and private, single site and multisite, profit and nonprofit, wide-ranging industries, and varied organizational structures. Over and over, the experiences were the same or very similar: certain recurring problems are rarely solved to the satisfaction of anyone.

During one particularly frustrating moment several years ago when I was seeing one of the rarely solved problems on the horizon, I wondered, *What would Jesus do?* Though He wasn't technically in the business field, did He have these types of problems? As I began to look more closely at His ministry, I realized, *Yes, He did.* Jesus, His disciples, prophets, and others had to deal with these same problems. Jesus encountered people who had strong and differing opinions, who had trouble making decisions, on and on. These problems persist today in professional and personal environments alike. So if these big-picture problems still exist, Jesus must have found solutions to handle them—and to offer satisfaction to all involved. Indeed, He did. And many of those solutions make up this book.

I want you to have outcomes different from the typically disastrous or at least troublesome ones you may encounter in your business environment. That's why in the following pages, I offer my insight as well as provide a look into how Jesus responded to help you have different and successful outcomes. Throughout the following chapters, we will identify each oft-occurring problem, provide biblical examples of processes that have been successful in addressing each problem, and present workable ideas from personal experience to support you in solving the unsolvable.

Engage the past, enable the present, and embolden the future with those who have been there and done that.

CHAPTER 1

RHETORIC TO RESULTS

For five years, I served as the vice president of student affairs for a community college in California. One of my responsibilities was to oversee its work experience program. Students in this program connected with local businesses that partnered with the college to provide experience in actual company environments that focused on the products or services the students were studying. Before each semester, I would visit the executives of each business to make sure that we were on the same page regarding their requirements and expectations for the students coming into their organization.

I expected the executives to talk about how they wanted to see high customer satisfaction ratings, speedy delivery for the product or service, strong team member participation, and other tangible and intangible skills. Instead, they wanted someone who could "At least write a simple memo," "Put a sentence together after answering the phone," "Say something that makes sense in a meeting," and "Listen to instructions."

I was stunned. Simply put, they wanted employees who could communicate clearly.

Why can't we conquer basic communication? Management experts such as John Adair, Mary Parker Follett, and John Maxwell have written books and chapters in books to explain the benefits of good business communication. These benefits include improved productivity, a positive atmosphere, enhanced loyalty to the company, and increased customer satisfaction. Who wouldn't want those benefits? And yet over and over, employers struggle to find employees who have achieved these qualities even after years of pursuing company projects, hiring college graduates with communication majors, spending vast amounts on consultants, and sending employees to endless seminars. Well-known businessman and consultant Peter Drucker was so exasperated about the failure of communication that he wrote in his book *Management,* "Can we then say anything constructive about communication? Can we do anything? … Our experience with communications—largely an experience of failure."[1]

But it doesn't have to be that way.

Consider the following invitation the president of a large, privately held manufacturing company emailed to the company's management.

> There will be a meeting of all department heads on Friday, January 8, at 6:00 p.m. in the company cafeteria. The purpose of this meeting is to review our year-end financials prior to their public release later in the month.
>
> Dinner will be served with the following options: steak, seafood, or vegetarian. If you have special dietary requirements, list those on your reply to this invitation. The dress expectation is business.
>
> Please respond to this invitation prior to December 30 with your ability to participate and your dinner choice. Thank you!

This president understood the power of clear communication. He focused on the message—that he expected employees to attend the dinner meeting on the date and time in business attire and prepared to hear the year-end financials of the organization in which they were leaders. He also understood the best method to use to reach his intended audience—email.

While it was a simple memo, it had a clear message and an effective method of delivery—communication that produced results. However, a review of this memo by today's memo gods would have resulted in several more menu and diet choices, a tease for the financial coming attraction, a timeline for the meeting in case someone had conflicts for the evening, and at least three means of responding. And as far as the distribution, most of the rest of the company would be copied on the email lest they feel slighted by not being included, a notice put in the company newsletter, and a copy placed on the lunchroom newsboard. What started out as simple and clear communication has in too many cases become complicated and ineffective.

Fortunately, we can get back to that simple and clear communication. Let's return to the basics. Forget all the bells and whistles that we can add, and focus only on two things: the *message* we want to communicate and the *method* we want to use to get that message to those who need to take action.

Two Elements of Communication That Lead to Success

In his email to the company's department heads, the president used the two elements of communication we mentioned above and successfully articulated his wants. Those two elements answered the following questions.

Message: What are you trying to say?

Method: How are you trying to say it? Are you writing and speaking, reading, listening and questioning, or offering nonverbals?

If we achieve success in these two elements, we will have arrived at a level of communication that produces positive results.

Message

We must make sure that those who receive our messages clearly understand them. If that does not happen, we have not communicated well. We, including those who send and those who receive, must hear the same message and understand the same actions to be taken, the priority expected, and the results to be achieved. Michael Hyatt, CEO of Michael Hyatt & Company, terms "hearing the same message" as "shared understanding."[2] Drucker calls it "shared experience."[3] Researchers and professors Judy Pearson and Paul Nelson refer to that kind of good communication as "the process of understanding and sharing meaning."[4]

Note that every definition includes the word *shared*. We may believe we are articulating clearly, but if the message fails to connect to the hearers—the people who are listening to us—do not have the same, or shared, understanding of what has been said—we have provided no communication. If there is no communication, there can be no accountability for actions or results.

At a company where I worked as a senior director, my boss continuously threw things on my desk with the instruction, "Handle this." He never offered a clue as to how I should handle it, the time frame for it, or who might be the most appropriate person to handle it. Nothing was shared in that communication. His handing out unclear and incomplete instructions led to frustration, delays, false starts, and built-up anxiety. The person who received the message could not understand it. Thus the message was not delivered; the action and accountability were not there. Communication failed.

If you want to communicate clearly and purposefully, first focus on the message itself. What do you want to say? In what way can you best say it? Have you offered a complete message free of assumptions? How will you know that the message was truly communicated? In what ways can you avoid being the bad "Handle it!" example?

The best shared messages rely on two key attributes: they must be *clear* and they must be *concise*. Though we could focus on many other attributes, if we make sure our messages are clear and concise, we will have put ourselves on the path to be truly heard.

Clarity

For a great example of clarity in communicating, let's consider the biblical story of Jesus entering Jerusalem knowing He was going to His crucifixion. Upon approaching the city,

> Jesus sent two disciples, saying to them, "Go to the village ahead of you, and at once you will find a donkey tied there, with her colt by her. Untie them and bring them to me. If anyone says anything to you, say the Lord needs them, and he will send them right away."

Then we see the response.

The disciples went and did as Jesus had instructed them. (Matthew 21:1–3, 6).

Jesus's words were bold, confident, straightforward, detailed, and very clear. He made it easy for His disciples to do what He wanted them to do even giving the response when the action was questioned.

The specific directives Jesus used to communicate to His disciples are ways we can be clear as we apply them to the messages we deliver today. And they will go a long way to alleviating frustration. Consider these ideas when formulating clear messages whether in writing or when speaking.

Know What You Want to Communicate

If you are not certain of what you want done and the expected results, how can you expect to accomplish shared understanding? Put yourself in the hearer's position and give yourself the message. Can you understand it, or are you making too many assumptions of understanding?

Jesus knew exactly what He wanted and answered the four key questions as He communicated to His disciples: what, why, when, and who.

- *What* you are doing gives a vision of the result you want achieved.
- *Why* is so important to building a relationship and a shared vision and objective. Be as transparent as is appropriate.
- *When* provides the timeline and due date for deliverables.
- *Who* presents those who will be involved and if appropriate in what roles.

Let's assume that the handle-it vice president wanted a meeting to discuss a new product. A message to the marketing team stating the following would be an example of clear communication.

> A new product is being added to our catalog for worldwide distribution [*what*], giving us a competitive entry into the international sales arena [*why*]. This product is due to be released on January 15 [*when*]. We will meet in building 10, conference room 201, on Tuesday, from 2:00 to 4:00 p.m. Please read the attached product description and marketing goals and come prepared with a preliminary plan for completing the responsibilities assigned to you [*who*] by July 30 or before.

The message is clear, complete, and unambiguous.

Write down what you want to say, and read it out loud to yourself. Ask yourself if you would know exactly what to do when you left the meeting or read the instructions. Would you know what you were accountable for and the timeline? Would you be ready to hit the ground running?

Ask for needed clarification. Always ask if any further information or additional details need to be released. Invite those who may be hesitant to speak out in a group to set up a time to meet with you individually.

Send follow-up notices. A summary of the communication highlights, an offer of help, a suggestion to reach out to those with specific skills where needed, a scheduled time to discuss progress, a friendly call or text, or any other appropriate notice should be sent to those involved in the original communication. Jack Welch talks about his constant reminders while the chairman and CEO at General Electric: "Whenever I had an idea or message I wanted to drive into the organization, I could never say it enough. I repeated it over and over and over, at every meeting and review."[5] That's clarity.

Conciseness

When sending the disciples to find the donkey, Jesus did not waste words getting to what He wanted: "Go to the village ahead of you, and at once you will find a donkey tied there, with her colt by her. Untie them and bring them to me." While this is clear, it's also concise. He didn't blather on and on, overexplaining. He got right to the point.

The Bible records other concise statements that convey a complete thought. Consider just these two: "Rejoice always" and "Pray continually" (1 Thessalonians 5:16–17).

My favorite concise statement from the Bible is John 3:16: "God so loved the world that he gave his one and only Son, that whoever believes in him shall not perish but have eternal life." In just one verse, Jesus offers the entire plan of salvation. How's that for being concise?

When Jesus communicated in longer passages, He still gave concise messages always completing a thought and then moving on from that topic to start another. He never rambled on from sentence to sentence in an attempt to keep the conversation going. Even at the end of the Sermon on the Mount, with adoring crowds clamoring for His continued discussions, we read, "When Jesus had finished saying these things, the crowds were amazed at his teaching ... When Jesus came down from the mountain, large crowds followed him" (Matthew 7:28, 8:1). Jesus had a golden opportunity to continue to impress the adoring crowds, but He "finished" and "came down from the mountain."

Consider these ideas when formulating concise written and spoken messages.

Doggedly edit your message. Each person reading or listening has a limited attention span; your message should have a limited number of points.

Practice your ending. Write and practice your closing when speaking so that you will not be tempted to ramble on when everything that needs to be said has been said. When an event continues after the objective has been met, it often degrades into a discussion that confuses and sometimes dilutes or even contradicts the results of the meeting.

Be careful of the question-and-answer period. If you are going to take questions at the end of a presentation, be deliberate about the number of questions you take and the time allowed for them. Entertain only questions that are specifically on the topics covered. If you rattle on in an impromptu session, you risk turning a clear message into a foggy translation.

Method

Jesus was an extremely competent and comprehensive communicator. His main methods of communicating were through speaking, listening, and offering nonverbal messages.

Unlike the limitations in Jesus's day, communication today goes way beyond those standards and presents a wide variety of methods by which we relay our messages. We can use everything from the simple pen and paper to elaborate applications that not only document our thoughts but also look for complementary sources for amplification. We communicate in the age-old reading, writing, and face-to-face manner or through any variety of electronic media with endless options for themes, backgrounds, sound accompaniments, and illustrations.

But behind all those options still lies the necessity of creating the most articulate *message* and finding the most effective *method* to deliver it. Let's look at four possible methods and combinations of methods for delivery: write and speak, read, listen and question, and nonverbal.

Write and Speak

When the scribes and Pharisees brought to Jesus a woman who had been caught in adultery, Jesus illustrated for us the *power* of writing. They told Jesus that Moses in the law had commanded that the woman be stoned and then asked Him what He would do. "This they said, testing Him, that they might have something of which to accuse Him. But Jesus stooped down and wrote on the ground with His finger, as though He did not hear" (John 8:6 NKJV). Although we have no record of what Jesus actually wrote, we know He did not just doodle. He wrote something powerful enough to cause the Pharisees to walk away.

Let's look at another example—This one shows us the *importance* of writing: "Go now, write it on a tablet for them, inscribe it on a scroll, that for the days to come it may be an everlasting witness" (Isaiah 30:8).

Speaking has traits very similar to those of writing. Let's look at the way Jesus spoke to see what we can glean from Him. He spoke to large groups, small groups, and individuals using a variety of styles and many parables (stories) to make sure everyone understood His message.

The Sermon on the Mount (Matthew 5–7), which Jesus preached to a large group, has been called "The Manifesto of the King."[6] That title is well deserved. In one epic sermon, the Beatitudes, starting each sentence with "Blessed is," identified the select groups of people—including the poor in spirit, the meek, the merciful, the pure in heart, and the peacemakers—who would experience genuine happiness and fulfillment. He helped His followers recognize the difference each could make in the world by talking about the salt of the earth and the light of the world. He taught them to pray effectively through the Lord's Prayer. He also addressed tough topics such as murder, adultery, boasting, and judging. He used many practical examples and stories to make sure everyone understood what He was saying in this memorable and groundbreaking sermon.

Jesus impressed a small group one Sabbath in the synagogue in Capernaum, and "the people were amazed at his teaching, because he taught them as one who had authority, not as the teachers of the law" (Mark 1:22).

And Jesus spoke to Nicodemus, an individual and member of the Jewish ruling council, one night when Nicodemus approached Him to get clarification regarding salvation and what being born again really meant. Jesus patiently addressed all his questions (see John 3:1–21). His answers to explain salvation and to respond to questions included John 3:16, which we mentioned earlier as a complete message in a single sentence.

As you write or speak as your method of choice, it's important to keep the following in mind.

Deliver your message. Your one objective is to come to a shared understanding of what you are relaying and your expectations of the audience.

Stress your goals, timelines, and expected results. If you delivered your message by speaking at a meeting or to a small group, follow up with a summary of the key objectives and expected results. Getting this in writing is critical. It will serve as objective accountability.

Use appropriate wording. When communicating in writing with friends or on social media, it may be fine to use "C U 2nite 4 🍽" for "See you tonight for dinner," but such cryptic wording is not appropriate for business and more-formal personal communication. Use standard wording, punctuation, and formatting when communicating in a professional environment.

Be prepared. While we have opportunity to review and edit written material, we have no do-overs in speaking. Once it comes out of our mouths, it firmly plants itself in the minds of those listening. How many times have we experienced a company or a well-known individual say something that had not been preapproved, was out of line, or was just plain wrong? The apologies and corrections come along predictably, but by then, it is too late; the message has been received and the damage done. Though we can attempt to defuse the impact of the statement, erasing it is not going to happen.

Check facts, check directives, check company information, and check all numbers. If you are unsure of something and have not been able to check it thoroughly, leave it out. Give your speech to a trusted friend or even to the mirror. Be sure it is what you want to relay as your message.

Use positive statements wherever possible. Jesus used positive words throughout the Sermon on the Mount: "Blessed are ..." And some translations even say, "Happy are ..." "Rejoice and be glad," "You are the light of the world," "Do not worry," and "Ask and it will be given to you." Everyone can use encouragement. You are asking for action. Building up people and purpose will create energy in that direction.

Watch the tone of your message. Remember that in written communications, people cannot interpret voice volume or subtle expressions as they can in speaking; consequently, the interpretation is left entirely up to the reader. Review carefully what you are writing to make sure the underlying tone cannot be misunderstood. Do not let your mood or a recent incident show up in your written communication or spoken message to the point that it can confuse or change the message's meaning.

Beware the question-and-answer period. As we mentioned previously with conciseness, it deserves an encore appearance here. Listen intently to questions people ask. Repeat or clarify the questions if necessary, and answer them directly. If you do not know the answer or are unable to answer, say that. Make sure you maintain control over the environment. Do not let it devolve into an unproductive, combative session. Always return to the agenda and the message.

Directly address tough topics. Try to identify the controversial topics that might arise in your speech or smaller group discussion, and prepare answers for those subjects. You need to use discretion and rely on your experience when addressing these topics. However, if you can at least acknowledge them, that will go a long way toward building trust with those listening. When speaking, address the issues and then move on.

Stay confident in chaos. This tip refers primarily to speaking opportunities. The many things that can and do go wrong in a meeting can impact even the most confident. Here are tips for keeping your cool and keeping your message and method on track.

- Make sure that the essential equipment and people are in place before you speak. Equipment, furnishings, and technology should all be where they need to be and be well tested.
- When the audience is large, make sure that the sound and projection systems are working, your presentation title slide is on the screen, your notes are in order on the podium, and those on the stage and in the audience are seated before you start to speak. We see a good example of this in the Sermon on the Mount, when Jesus walked up on the mountain, sat, and waited for His disciples to arrive before He started speaking. He did not fidget, get up to talk to someone, or rustle through His notes (see Matthew 5:1–2).

- For a small gathering, though you may not have to worry about the sound and slide systems, the same warning applies—Have everyone in the room and ready to participate in the meeting.
- No matter the size, when problems arise such as technical people fooling around with the various systems, not having enough copies for everyone in attendance, the computer screen not showing on the stage screen, the microphone cracking and cutting out, or someone calling loudly to see if a missing attendee is on the way—that is the time to remain quiet and confident.
- If a problem appears not to have a solution within an acceptable time frame, you may have no choice but to dismiss and reschedule the meeting. However, mitigating actions could include doing the best you can with a basic outline and telling your audience that you will send out a summary of key points.

Read

Jesus was born into the family of a carpenter, a family not of the educated class who would have learned to read. Yet the gospel of Luke makes it clear that Jesus amazed them all by His concise actions.

> He went to Nazareth, where He had been brought up, and on the Sabbath day he went into the synagogue, as was his custom. He stood up to read, and the scroll of the prophet Isaiah was handed to him. Unrolling it, he found the place where it was written ... Then he rolled up the scroll, gave it back to the attendant and sat down. The eyes of everyone in the synagogue were fastened on Him. (Luke 4:16–17, 20)

Reading is an important method of getting across our message. I grew up in a family of readers. My mother read to me at bedtime, family members all participated in reading from the Bible during daily devotions at the breakfast table, and my parents made sure that books were always available.

That is all well and good, you might be saying, but how does that fit into communication? You may think that the only thing communicating to you when reading is a bunch of words. And you might be more interested in listening to podcasts than wading through piles of written stuff. And yet reading requires focus that absorbs you into the setting and action; many beautiful word pictures fill your mind, and the many different ways of expressing feelings and fears are worth the effort to add a window of time to your schedule for reading.

In addition to personal enjoyment, you reap many benefits of reading that directly impact communication. Let's look at a few.

Knowledge. Everything you read puts new information in your mind. You never know when that information will come in handy. Current events that impact your organization or industry, community news, innovative and creative ideas, leisure activities, and many other bits of information will be welcomed in varied situations and with various types of professional and personal individuals and groups.

Vocabulary. The more you read, the more words you are exposed to both as words themselves and as familiar words in new contexts. For example, the simple word *read* will be more descriptive when you see *peruse* or *scrutinize* or even *devour*, such as "I *devoured* the contents of the new book on mountain climbing." The words and use of words you see in your reading will start showing up in your writing and speaking. Remember, it is always an asset to be well read, articulate, and knowledgeable on a variety of topics.

Focus and concentration. Our attention is drawn in a million different directions as we multitask. In a small window of time, we will check email, respond to texts, work on tasks, check social media, and interact with coworkers. Reading requires that we focus on the material. Even if we are skimming for specific information, we are focused.

Entertainment and relaxation. There is a reading genre for everyone. It may be classical literature, poetry, targeted-subject magazines, biographies, self-help guides, science fiction, romance novels, or mysteries. You are sure to find something out there to capture your attention if you look for it.

Listen and Question

Listening and questioning are very important elements of communication. We listen to understand. We question to clarify. We elevate the importance of the person with whom we are interacting by listening and questioning. We can find many examples of Jesus's building relationships and communicating clearly through these methods.

In the first book of the Bible, Jesus listened to Rachel regarding her inability to have children: "Then God remembered Rachel, and God listened to her" (Genesis 30:22 NASB).

The Lord listened to His heavenly Father in prayer: "Very early in the morning, while it was still dark, Jesus got up, left the house and went off to a solitary place, where he prayed" (Mark 1:35).

Jesus even nudged others to listen: "Jesus called the crowd to him and said, 'Listen and understand'" and "Consider carefully how you listen" (Matthew 15:10; Luke 8:18). He often talked about listening; after a message, He would say, "Whoever has ears, let them hear."

But He didn't just listen. He actively questioned. Consider these examples.

During a discussion about the temple tax, Jesus asked Peter, "What do you think?" (Matthew 17:25).

At the end of one of their days of travel, Jesus asked His disciples, "Who do people say the Son of Man is?" The disciples answered with John the Baptist, Elijah, Jeremiah, or one of the prophets. Jesus pressed them by asking, "But what about you? … Who do you say that I am?" Peter then answered, "You are the Messiah, the Son of the living God" (Matthew 16:13–16).

Jesus encountered two people on the road to Emmaus on the day He had risen from the grave. These two did not recognize Jesus, who was walking with them as they discussed all the things that had gone on in Jerusalem. Jesus asked them, "What are you discussing together as you walk along?" One of them, named Cleopas, told Jesus He must be the only one in Jerusalem who did not know the things that had happened. Jesus pressed, "What things?" The two told Him about His own crucifixion and the rumor that He was missing from the grave and that some had seen a vision that He was alive. Jesus continued to question and discuss until the eyes of the two were opened and they recognized that they were talking to Him (Luke 24:13–31).

But how do we listen and ask questions to help us communicate well?

Listen objectively. Keep an open mind as you listen to different opinions. Think about how we often interact today. We see conversations that barely get started before another person interrupts with his or her point of view. When questions come up, someone starts attacking before the other person gets a chance to utter even a sentence. Popular television programs are based on overlapping and usually loud exchanges. Interacting in a rude or uncaring manner will shut down any communication with the other party or parties.

Listen attentively. Jesus did not let His busy calendar and His long to-do list distract Him from listening. He looked at people. He focused on the conversation. He let them know that they mattered. Give the person or group your full attention. Look at them; talk directly to them. Show people how important they and their ideas are by giving them your undivided attention.

Ask for clarification or additional details. Ask questions that will usually elicit more than a one- or two-word answer. "Tell me more about that." "Why was that action taken?" "What would you see as the next step?"

Make clear your use of the information from the questions and answers. A warning here is to make sure as you engage by asking questions that the participants know you will take all the information you gather into consideration but may not choose to go in the direction they suggest. Too often, those expressing differing opinions think that once you hear the truth as they know it, you will obviously change course and go their way.

Nonverbal: Facial and Action Expressions

Nothing would stop me in my tracks—whether at the dinner table, a birthday celebration, or a church meeting—than *that look* from my mother. I would guess that many have similar memories. We also can see many examples of that look throughout the Bible.

- God noted Cain's anger by the look on his face. "Why are you angry? Why is your face downcast?" (Genesis 4:5–6).
- The Lord punished the king of Assyria for his haughty looks. "I will punish the king of Assyria for the willful pride of his heart and the haughty look in his eyes" (Isaiah 10:12).
- Jesus gave instructions to His disciples before He sent them out to carry on the ministry He had started. Among those instructions was a physical sign for those who did not accept them. "If anyone will not welcome you or listen to your words, leave that home or town and shake the dust off your feet" (Matthew 10:14).
- Jesus was angry at the Pharisees regarding their law about not healing anyone on the Sabbath. "He looked around at them in anger and, deeply distressed at their stubborn hearts" (Mark 3:5).

- Jesus looked at Peter right after he had denied Him three times causing Peter to weep. "The Lord turned and looked straight at Peter. Then Peter remembered the word the Lord had spoken to him: 'Before the rooster crows today, you will disown me three times.' And he went outside and wept bitterly" (Luke 22:61–62).

Be attentive to facial and bodily expressions. Sometimes, facial and bodily expressions are almost automatic. Make a point to change that. Be conscious of your expressions and deliberate in their use. Smirking, rolling your eyes, looking and acting bored, tidying your desk, stretching, waving at someone walking by, continually checking your phone—These actions indicate a lack of interest and will be interpreted as your lack of interest in the person or persons and the topic(s).

Provide positive affirmations. Smiling, nodding, focusing on the person or persons indicate interest and will create a positive atmosphere where everyone can share ideas. Be conscious of your facial expressions and actual action. Nonverbal actions can speak louder than words.

Nonverbal: Silence

Jesus used silence at a crucial time in His life. In all four Gospels (Matthew 27:12, Mark 15:5, Luke 23:9, and John 19:9), the writers noted that Jesus spoke not a word when Pilate questioned Him about the accusations the chief priests and elders had brought to him. Jesus was sure to be crucified if He presented no defense, and yet He kept silent.

Jesus also used silence to be quiet and pray to His heavenly Father. As His fame grew throughout Galilee, "crowds of people came to hear him and to be healed of their sicknesses" (Luke 5:16). Jesus was famous. How did He handle His success? As Luke reported, He "would withdraw to desolate places and pray" (5:16 ESV).

Then there is a time when Peter should have been silent.

> Jesus took Peter, James and John with him and
> led them up a high mountain, where they were all
> alone. There he was transfigured before them. His
> clothes became dazzling white, whiter than anyone
> in the world could bleach them. And there appeared
> before them Elijah and Moses who were talking
> with Jesus. (Mark 9:2–4)

The disciples were scared. They did not know what to say. But
that didn't stop Peter. He blurted out, "Let us put up three shelters—
one for you, one for Moses and one for Elijah." At that moment, a
cloud appeared, and the voice of God said, "This is my Son, whom I
love. Listen to him!" (Mark 9:5–7). Peter was graciously spared from
any more chatter, and others were spared from having to respond
to Peter.

Matthew and Mark provided a parenthetical excuse for Peter:
"He did not know what to say, they were so frightened" (Matthew
17:6; Mark 9:6). When Peter recorded this experience in 2 Peter
1:16–18, he wisely omitted his part. Most of us can relate to Peter;
we remember times when words not thought through tumbled
out of our mouths and resulted in undesirable consequences and
embarrassment. As Ecclesiastes 3:7 wisely reminds us, there is "a
time to keep silent, and a time to speak."

So how does silence help our method of getting out a shared
message?

Silence is an important aspect of communication. You don't need
to think that you must fill every moment with chatter. As Willy
Steiner states,

> In communicating, it's been shown that words
> account for 10% of what's expressed, vocal tone
> and pace 35%, and nonverbal communication

a whopping 55%. Silence is a critical aspect of nonverbal communication and ... vastly underutilized. You can say a lot by saying nothing.[7]

Use silence as a tool. Silence can add importance to what was just said or is about to be said and to silently challenge others to respond.

Take time for yourself. When needed, retreat from the overloaded schedule for rest, reflection, and prayer.

Stop talking. When you have nothing to say, say nothing.

Red-Screen Rhetoric

A corporation in the forest products industry retained my company to set up an executive information system. This system produced reports for key indicators such as revenues by product line, advertising expenses, and employee turnover, and it showed the results in red, yellow, or green depending on how the actual figures related to the goals the corporation had set. For example, if an executive was in charge of sales, the report might produce sales figures by product for each geographic region. If they were close to their target goal, the numbers would be green, but if they were way off the mark, the numbers would be red.

Our team was almost finished with the identification of key indicators and the corresponding goals when we met with the vice president of operations. We opened by explaining the process and the need for identifying the items to be reported as well as the established goals. The VP said,

> Stop right there. No way am I going to fiddle around with colored numbers. If there is anything in my area that has a problem, just turn my entire screen red. The minute I see that, I will tear out of this office. And the managers in my divisions better know what is wrong and be well on their way to fixing it.

How much simpler could communication get? A message that said "trouble" distributed by a method that was one red computer screen. The *message* was clear, the *method* was effective, and the desired *results* were achieved. This is possible for all of us. We can get back to the basics and change the history of failure in communication. It's worth the effort.

CHAPTER 2
TEAMS THAT WORK

During the Vietnam War, Charles Plumb, a US Navy jet pilot, flew seventy-five combat missions before his plane was destroyed by a surface-to-air missile. Though Plumb ejected successfully, he parachuted into enemy hands; he spent six years in a communist Vietnamese prison.

Plumb survived and returned to his family. One day as Plumb and his wife were eating in a restaurant, a man at another table said, "Charles Plumb!" and came up to his table. He excitedly commented that Plumb had flown jet fighters in Vietnam from the aircraft carrier *Kitty Hawk* and that he had been shot down.

"How in the world do you know all of that?" Plumb asked the man.

"I packed your parachute," the man replied.[8]

What a great team that was! I'm sure at one time or another, you have been fortunate to see teams that were successful and worked together to achieve amazing things. Not sure? Have you ever watched the Macy's Thanksgiving Day parade or the Super Bowl?

I have worked extensively in the health care industry throughout my consulting career and have seen clear examples of teams in hospitals, generally led by doctors, who were mobilized to provide the services patients needed. Each person on the team took personal responsibility for the team's success. The core teams worked well together, and they drew on the whole organization as needed bringing in laboratory technicians in one stage, radiologists in another phase, and physical therapists at still another point. While the team skills could be different for each patient, the responsibility of the team was always the same: to successfully provide treatment. Everyone understood his or her role and needed to contribute at a high level in that role to bring about the success of the team. When a hospital team did not function as expected, the stakes were high and the results were obvious—and sometimes deadly.

Unfortunately, most of us have also come in contact with or have been on teams that did not work. The time I spent teaching in the graduate program at a California university comes to mind when I think of the frustration of teams that do not work. The primary project for each class was an assignment that required the students to work in teams. The teams could self-select or be assigned by the two of us who were jointly teaching this course. No matter how they were originally formed, the teams were almost always failures at working together. One team member would do most of the work, another team member would tattle about how no one listened to her or his ideas, still another wanted to finish the project as a solo effort, or a very busy team member managed to miss every team working session. We would do our best as instructors to get teams together and back on track, but neither of us could claim a high level of success at that.

Clearly, the hospital teams and the university teams included talented members. What was the difference between them? Why was one successful and able to deliver while the other failed and disappointed? When we can figure out the answers to those questions and put them to work for us, we will set ourselves up for success to deliver expected results through teams that work.

Teams Are Problematic and Powerful

Teams are very powerful because of their makeup and objectives, but that same makeup can contribute to the problematic side. How could that be when the small number of team members, each with different but complementary skills, are all focused on accomplishing a common objective? That sounds fantastic until you think that each team member is likely a star in her or his specific area. Each member is coming at the objective from a different direction with self-discipline and self-motivation powering the progress. Then you have a leader who is tasked with keeping the team members on track and on schedule, dealing with the conflicts that naturally surface, and doing all of this without the authority of a boss. What could possibly go wrong? Enough for Peter Drucker to observe, "Teams fail—and the failure rate has been high."[9] A team structure does add risk to the accomplishment of an objective, but we must not let the problems of the team overshadow the power of the team.

The power of the team comes from that same makeup—highly skilled members focused on attaining an objective that is key to the success of the entire organization. With that power, a team can accomplish much more than an individual ever could. In *Jesus on Leadership,* C. Gene Wilkes shares reasons why teams are superior to individual efforts.

- Teams involve more people, thus affording more resources, ideas, and energy than would an individual.
- Teams maximize a leader's potential and minimize her weaknesses. Strengths and weaknesses are more exposed in individuals.
- Teams provide multiple perspectives of how to meet a need or reach a goal, thus devising several alternatives for each situation. Individual insight is seldom as broad and deep as a group's when it takes on a problem.
- Teams share the credit for victories and the blame for losses. This fosters genuine humility and authentic community. Individuals take credit and blame alone. This fosters pride and sometimes a sense of failure.
- Teams keep leaders accountable for the goal. Individuals connected to no one can change the goal without accountability.
- Teams can simply do more than an individual.[10]

Keeping a strong focus on the common objective throughout the entire process can reduce the risk of the problems in a team structure and increase the likelihood of its success.

Why Did Jesus Need a Team?

Jesus was successful doing most of His early work as a single shingle in the rural villages and hillsides of Galilee, but then He wanted to work with a team because He knew that the time for His ministry on earth was limited. He had successfully spread His message to a geographical area, but He would soon be gone. He needed people to carry on His message and spread it throughout the world. Jesus needed a team.

Scottish theologian A. B. Bruce points out in his classic work *The Training of the Twelve* when and why Jesus identified and called the twelve apostles from the larger group of His followers.

> The selection by Jesus of the twelve from the band of disciples who had gradually gathered around His person, is an important landmark in the Gospel history. It divides the ministry of our Lord into two portions, nearly equal probably as to duration, but unequal as to the extent and importance of the work done in each respectively. In the earlier period Jesus laboured single-handed; His miraculous deeds were confined for the most part to a limited area; and His teaching was in the main of an elementary character. But by the time when the twelve were chosen, the work of the gospel had assumed such dimensions as to require organization and division of labour; and the teaching of Jesus was beginning to be of a deeper and more elaborate nature, and His gracious activities were taking on ever-widening range.[11]

Jesus had a clear objective and knew when He could work individually and when He could best use a team. The same needs to be true of us. When would it be better for us to go it alone, and when should we use a team? Let's look at the following characteristics that should be present before deciding to put a team together.

The Objective Requires Multiple Functions

If the hierarchical organization needs to mobilize multiple functions to address a common objective, that is a good time to enlist a team. Consider the airline industry. Everyone who works for an airline has to perform his or her assigned role to get a passenger from one location to another by way of a flight.

Accomplishing this objective requires individuals from each functional area to work as a team that then feeds results to the ultimate decision: fly or not fly. Airline administrative efforts make sure the names of everyone on the flight are recorded and payment has been received; maintenance makes sure the plane is flight worthy; operations get planes and crews where they need to be; ground crews get the plane parked, luggage to the carousel, and planes back out to the runway; crews get passengers to their destinations safely; weather experts identify risks in the filed flight plan; and airline flight controllers watch the flight from the time it leaves the gate at the departure terminal to when it is turned over to the airport flight controllers at its destination. The entire airline must be filled with efficient and effective functional teams that provide the direction to the ultimate decision made by the flight team. Airline flights have multifunctional demands.

The Objective Requires Interdependent Tasks

Do team members depend on one another to get information, support, or materials from other team members to make decisions or to be effective in other ways? In the airline example, each team provides its approval to proceed to the next step. For the hospital, the anesthesiologist during a surgery will alert the team if the patient's organ functions deviate from normal, will advise them on what to do, and will let them know when they can return to their expected roles and activities.

Common Objective

No matter the composition, the team needs to have a powerful, motivating objective that every member can understand and strive to accomplish. For the hospital, it is to provide the services needed for an individual patient, and for the airline, it is to transport a passenger from one location to another via a flight.

Building a Team That Works

Jesus needed not only a team; He needed one that worked. There was no plan B. He staked everything on His team of apostles. Fortunately, Jesus was a master team builder; He developed twelve ordinary men into a team that carried His message to the ends of the earth.

Who were these twelve apostles? Andrew, Simon Peter, James, and John worked as fishermen (Matthew 4:18–22). Thomas, Nathaniel (Bartholomew), and Philip may have also worked as fishermen for they were fishing all together when Jesus appeared to them following His resurrection (John 21:2–8). Matthew, called Levi in Luke, worked as a tax collector for the Roman government, a position despised by the general population (Luke 5:27). Simon was a zealot engaged in a political group attempting to overthrow the Roman government (Luke 6:15). The Bible does not tell us what Judas Iscariot—identified in each of the Gospels as the one who betrayed Jesus—did prior to becoming an apostle. Likewise with

Thaddaeus and James (son of Alphaeus) though they were probably tradesmen or craftsmen before becoming followers of Christ. There you have it—four and possibly seven fishermen, a tax collector, a political zealot, two possible tradesmen, and a traitor.

Just from their work resumes, it may be difficult to imagine this assembled team being able to work well or even get along. Imagine receiving this (tongue-in-cheek) memo from a consulting company regarding an assessment of the apostles' qualifications.

To: Jesus, Son of Joseph

Woodcrafter's Carpenter Shop

Nazareth 25922

From: Jordan Management Consultants

Dear Sir:

Thank you for submitting the resumes of the twelve men you have picked for managerial positions in your new organization. All of them have now taken our battery of tests; and we have not only run the results through our computer but also have arranged personal interviews for each of them with our psychologist and vocational aptitude consultant.

The profiles of all tests are included, and you will want to study each of them carefully.

As part of our service, we make some general comments for your guidance, much as an auditor will include some general statements. This is given as a result of staff consultation and comes without any additional fee.

It is the staff opinion that most of your nominees are lacking in background, education, and vocational aptitude for the type of enterprise you are undertaking. They do not have the team concept. We would recommend that you continue your search for persons of experience in managerial ability and proven capability.

Simon Peter is emotionally unstable and given to fits of temper. Andrew has absolutely no qualities of leadership. The two brothers, James and John, the sons of Zebedee, place personal interest above company loyalty. Thomas demonstrates a questioning attitude that would tend to undermine morale. We feel that it is our duty to tell you that Matthew had been blacklisted by the Greater Jerusalem Better Business Bureau; James, the son of Alphaeus, and Thaddaeus definitely have radical leanings, and they both registered a high score on the manic-depressive scale.

One of the candidates, however, shows great potential. He is a man of ability and resourcefulness, meets people well, has a keen business mind, and has contacts in high places. He is highly motivated, ambitious, and responsible. We recommend Judas Iscariot as your controller and right-hand man. All of the other profiles are self-explanatory.

We wish you every success in your new venture.[12]

In *Twelve Ordinary Men,* John MacArthur sums up the challenge for Jesus and His disciples.

Think about the ramifications of this: From our human perspective, the propagation of the gospel and the founding of the church hinged entirely on twelve men whose most outstanding characteristic was their ordinariness.[13]

These twelve were not the obvious choice for a successful team. To complicate the team-building task even more, by the time Jesus called these twelve ordinary men from the larger group of His followers, His earthly ministry, which was only about three years, was already half over.[14] The disciples had slightly more than eighteen months of training for the monumental task of spreading the gospel message.

How did Jesus build this team? Let's look at the key ingredients that went into developing the twelve apostles and should go into our steps for developing a team that works.

Consulting with God

The first thing Jesus did in the process of choosing His disciples was to ask His Father for advice: "Jesus went out to a mountainside to pray, and spent the night praying to God" (Luke 6:12). The decision regarding who would carry the gospel forward was a huge decision, and Jesus wanted to make sure His Father was involved: "When morning came, he called his disciples to him and chose twelve of them, whom he also designated apostles" (Luke 6:13).

Pray for guidance. Jesus always waits to hear from us and wants to be involved in all we do. It isn't hard to figure out that asking for God's help should be the first thing we do in selecting our team members, but asking for God's guidance should be a habit throughout every day and for all of the decisions we make.

Inspiring Objective

An objective inspires passion and builds commitment for the long haul. The beginning of any venture, kickoff meeting and all, is very exciting. The end with the congratulatory celebration is also energy filled. But … the middle can be a bear with discouraging times, deadlines missed, and conflict within and outside the team. The key to renewed commitment during these times is to focus on the objective.

Jesus had a clear objective when He selected the twelve apostles and started their training. It has become known as the Great Commission.

> All authority in heaven and on earth has been given to me. Therefore go and make disciples of all nations, baptizing them in the name of the Father and of the Son and of the Holy Spirit, and teaching them to obey everything I have commanded you. (Matthew 28:18–20)

The key words are *make disciples.* This inspiring directive became the driving passion of their lives. That passion and the influence of the Holy Spirit saw the apostles through persecution, rejection, and suffering. It even carried them through a very dark period on the night Jesus was betrayed by Judas (Matthew 26:49).

On that night, Jesus's trusted apostles scattered like sheep who had no shepherd (see Matthew 26:31). Peter actually denied three times that he even knew Jesus (Matthew 26:69–75). Even after the crucifixion and resurrection, the apostles seemed unsure of themselves, some even going back to their former day jobs in fishing boats (John 21:1–3).

But the passion and the courage returned in full force with the Holy Spirit. Sense the excitement in this passage from Luke.

> After the Lord Jesus had spoken to them, he was taken up into heaven and he sat at the right hand of God. Then the disciples went out and preached everywhere, and the Lord worked with them and confirmed his word by the signs that accompanied it. (Mark 16:19–20)

MacArthur succinctly states the unmeasurable impact of the apostles: "Those men, through the legacy of New Testament Scripture and the testimony they left, are still changing the world even today."[15] The objective Jesus set and the power of the Holy Spirit served to drive the apostles to the desired outcome.

The hospital and the airline both have inspiring and action-driving objectives. But even with these exciting end goals, getting to them can have low points. Let's look at some tips to reducing the drudgery we may find in the middle of any team effort.

Break into short phases the path to the objective accomplishment. Your team will still have to endure that boring middle time between starting and completing, but you can shorten that boring middle time by having more deliverables. Jesus broke the training up into three basic phases: train, practice what was learned, and participate in more-advanced training (Mark 3:14; Luke 9:1–10). Success energizes. Shorter times between objectives will give more wins and more positive energy.

Continually train and support. Remember that the whole team—not any individual on that team—is responsible for the result. The more experienced members need to help those who are newer to the process and perhaps not as seasoned in the skill set required. This support needs to go beyond specific skills to teach the team members how to deal with one another, successfully handle disagreements, give credit where it is due, and communicate in a positive manner.

Very important, Jesus did not stop guiding the apostles after He was crucified; He continued to mentor them even after they deserted Him on the night He was betrayed, after the resurrection, and after some of the discouraged apostles had returned to fishing. Jesus patiently called them from their boats, served them a breakfast of bread and fish, and encouraged them by once again saying, "Follow me" (John 21:4–19).

Pursuing Effective Leadership

Jesus was a great leader. He had completed His mission as He stated in John 17:4: "I have brought you glory on earth by finishing the work you gave me to do." He had not only trained the disciples but had also trained a leader to succeed Him with the apostles. What leader had He picked? The apostle with the greatest possibility to let his mouth start moving before his mind was engaged—Peter. MacArthur summarized Peter's time in training.

> Peter's name is mentioned in the Gospels more than any other name except Jesus. No one speaks as often as Peter, and no one is spoken to by the Lord as often as Peter. No disciple is so frequently rebuked by the Lord as Peter; and no disciple ever rebukes the Lord except Peter (Matthew 16:22). No one else confessed Christ more boldly or acknowledged His lordship more explicitly; yet no other disciple ever verbally denied Christ as forcefully or as publicly as Peter did. No one is praised and blessed by Christ the way Peter was; yet Peter was also the only one Christ ever addressed as Satan. The Lord had harsher things to say to Peter than He ever said to any of the others.

> All of that contributed to making him the leader Christ wanted him to be. God took a common man with an ambivalent, vacillating, impulsive,

unsubmissive personality and shaped him into a rocklike leader—the greatest preacher among the apostles.[16]

What can we glean from how Jesus brought Peter around to being a forceful leader in carrying out His mission?

Leadership needs to be strong. A team is not a hierarchical structure; it is a group of people with complementary skills who are working toward a common objective. No one has authority over anyone else. No one is responsible or can take credit for achieving the desired result. All the members are equally responsible; the team operates as a unit. The leader is the key to assuring that all the members understand their contribution, the skills they are bringing to the table, and their responsibility for producing deliverables on schedule. The clarification of responsibility also applies to the leader. When a variance from the assigned responsibility occurs or the product is not in line with what is expected, it is up to the leader to step in and make those corrections.

Look for the raw material. Do not focus on the quiet members of a group who never cause trouble, never ask the tough questions, and never create waves; they will not get out in front and lead the charge for action and results.

Note that the apostles naturally followed Peter after the resurrection when they were feeling confused. Peter, Thomas, Nathaniel, and two other apostles were together when Peter said, "I'm going out to fish," and the others responded, "We'll go with you" (John 21:3). I always say that I would rather slow people down or nudge them back onto the path than to have to push them every step of the way.

Be patient. Training the apostles was not an easy process. Jesus Himself made statements such as, "Are you still so dull?" (Matthew 15:16). "Do you not yet understand?" (Matthew 16:9). "How foolish you are, and how slow to believe" (Luke 24:25). Though the twelve were frustrating at times, Jesus kept mentoring, encouraging, patiently instructing, and providing them with ministry opportunities. Even after Peter had denied Jesus three times and decided to go back to fishing after the resurrection, Jesus did not give up. He specifically asked Peter to "feed my sheep" (John 21:17). We all need to ramp up our patience and keep on mentoring, raising each team member to a new level of competence.

Encourage. Truett Cathy, the founder of Chick-fil-A, famously said on many occasions, "How do you know if someone needs encouraging? If they are breathing."[17] No one tires of encouraging words. Make sure you are liberal with your encouragement to balance out the corrections and redirection that will need to be part of mentoring.

Possessing Dedicated Team Members

Jesus required the apostles to be dedicated to Him and His objective. We can see the dedication required by His call to Simon Peter and his fishing buddies. After fishing all night and catching nothing, Jesus asked Peter to launch out into the deep and lower his nets. Peter obeyed, and the result was a catch that overwhelmed their nets and nearly sank two of their fishing boats (Luke 5:4–7). Right after that, Jesus said, "Come, follow me … and I will send you out to fish for people" (Matthew 4:19). This is the point where "they pulled their boats up on shore, left everything and followed him" (Luke 5:11).

What can we learn from Jesus and His selection of the apostles to our process of finding members for a team that works?

Start recruiting from the minute the team is formed. When we meet with the executives to solicit support, we need to stress the importance of the project to them. Generalizing benefits will not do it; they need to know how the results of the team's effort will specifically benefit them and their department or unit. Once they see the "What's in it for me?" they will be more willing to recommend team members from their areas who will be strong in their commitment to the team and willing to take on the responsibility. Without commitment, the executives will think about what persons they will miss the least for the duration of the team effort. They certainly will not recommend their star players.

In *Jack: Straight from the Gut,* Jack Welch, former CEO and chairman of the board of General Electric, talked about the difficulty of getting top-notch people on a project team: "No one wants to give up their best talent on a full-time basis. They've got high targets to reach and need their best managers to make them."[18]

Control the size of the team. The size question has been asked for more than 150 years dating back to 1861, when Maximilian Ringelmann, a French agricultural engineer discovered that the more people who pulled on a rope, the less effort each individual contributed.[19] Most of the ideas about team size today focus on sports team and come up with an ideal team size of anywhere from five to fifteen members (Gaelic football has fifteen in case you were wondering). Businessman, consultant, and author Peter Drucker talks about team size in *Management.*

> The *greatest limitation* of the team structure is *size.* Teams work best when there are few members ... seven to fifteen members ... If a team gets much larger, it becomes unwieldy. Its strengths—such as flexibility and the sense of responsibility of the members—diminish.[20]

Stress contribution and accountability. The effective team member will focus on contributing—looking toward the objective. Contribution forces a responsibility for results rather than just effort. A team does not have a hierarchical design or the authority that goes with positions in that design. Team members need to rethink their laser focus on specific skills or specialties and think instead of how these skills and specialties can contribute to the performance and results of the team. Communication is now sideways instead of up and down. The team wins or the team loses.

Report progress honestly. How many teams report that they are on target when they are actually behind? Often, they think they can catch up. Other times, they are afraid of the expected consequences. Report the actual progress your team has made including reasons the tasks are not on schedule or over budget. If you shade the results, the consequences can snowball.

Communicate regularly with the department or unit managers who provided team members. Give them updates. Tell them how thankful you are for the resources they contributed. Remind them that you will give them performance reviews for the persons they have on the team. Keep them on your side.

Provide temporary stand-ins for the departments that have contributed members to the team. Whenever possible, shore up the missing skill. A client of mine did that very successfully by reaching out to those who held similar positions but had retired or who had elected not to return from maternity leave. The remuneration for those filling in needs to be attractive, and the department and the team member will greatly appreciate the effort and expense.

Augment from the outside only if your team requires special skills. When you bring in outsiders, you are saying that the selected team members cannot do the job. This can disappoint the insiders and isolate the outsider. Bite the dollar bullet and pay for the specialist to attend all meetings and events with the team. This will create the cohesiveness needed for the team to be successful. Jesus knew He needed someone to shoulder the load of carrying the gospel to the wider Roman Empire. He went outside of His chosen twelve and picked Paul to be the "apostle to the Gentiles" (Romans 11:13).

Offer options if team members' being totally dedicated is not a realistic expectation. While this should not be a starting point, you will encounter times when it is not feasible to expect full-time participation by key members of the team. I was the manager for a large project that was to convert all the health records in a hospital with over four hundred beds to a new system. This system not only touched every single department in the hospital but also impacted the health care professionals who practiced there by extending access to the system from their individual offices. Putting together a totally dedicated small core team was possible, but it was not possible to get full-time involvement from all of the skills and specialties needed. The option that worked well during this entire project was to have no scheduled team activities on Mondays. That allowed planning for appointments with those whose input was essential while still being considerate of time commitments.

This team organization worked because though not everyone could be fully committed time wise, everyone was dedicated to the project. Every team member and his or her representative area could see how the system would make their jobs simpler, the data more accurate, and the records immediately accessible. Commitment was the key to success.

Do not play down the commitment that is required, a temptation when attempting to get those top-of-the-line team members. John Maxwell, founder of the John Maxwell Leadership Foundation, has this to say about the importance of commitment: "Without each person's conviction that the cause is worth the price, the battle will never be won, and the team will not succeed. There must be commitment."[21]

Offering Performance Expectations and Rewards

Jesus promised His apostles the reward of all rewards in response to Peter's question: "We have left everything to follow you! What then will there be for us?" (Matthew 19:27). Jesus told them,

> Truly I tell you, at the renewal of all things, when the Son of Man sits on his glorious throne, you who have followed me will also sit on twelve thrones,

judging the twelve tribes of Israel. And everyone who has left houses or brothers or sisters or father or mother or wife or children or fields for my sake will receive a hundred times as much and will inherit eternal life. (Matthew 19:28–29)

No way will we come even close to offering such a wonderful reward for the success of our team members! But let's look at what options are available to let them know we care.

Small rewards are exciting. The time in the middle of any team effort often gets tiring, disappointing, and discouraging, so expect it and plan for it. I used to give small, branded items to each team member that related to an upcoming focus event—a calculator that represented a concern over the cost overrun, a calendar marked with the end date of the team effort, a USB drive as a symbol of the data conversion phase, and so on. Though these were low-cost elements, the team was always pleased to receive them. And getting a gift is always a good thing.

Group events. Get the team away for a fun time that has nothing to do with the team effort. How about an indoor beach party? A competitive race with bumper cars? An art or cooking class? The team will build rapport and be more energized to return to the team efforts.

Day off. This is not always possible in every organization, but any team loves a day off … no strings attached.

Let's Go Live

A mid-sized Christian university, which was my client, put together a team that was connected, confident, dedicated, determined, and truly a one for all and all for one group. They formed this team with the objective of moving from a simple database (where all the data for all university functions were stored in simple records) to a complex database that would facilitate growth, search, and flexibility. This was a monumental effort even if they'd had all the time in the world.

But they did not have that time luxury. The team, with support from the executives, decided to convert to the new data structure on January 1. That date would eliminate many additional tasks that would need to be completed to convert payroll anytime other than at the start of the year. This gave them exactly five and a half months to pull it off. The team took on that challenge with gusto. They worked unbelievable hours and adhered to all the plans and processes especially when it came to testing and user education. The users reacted positively to the enthusiasm and got on board.

December arrived with the team still in the testing, modifying, and testing again phase. They were confident that they could make it by their deadline, and their enthusiasm was contagious. In the middle of December, the client's accounting firm, which was one of the major players, wrote a long, detailed opinion letter about its rejection of the cutover for January 1. That injected a huge risk for the university about that conversion date.

December 30 saw the team having tested each of the separate pieces of the new system but not having tested the latest changes in the complete, integrated process. The team had done everything they could to mitigate the risk such as backups of all data for several days back, reviewing repeatedly the unit tests, and seeking the support of the users. Decision time was here.

The team and many of the users had prayed all night for guidance about what they should do. In the morning, they told me they wanted to convert to the new system on January 1 and were sure that was the right direction. I reminded them of the risk and the consequential time-consuming actions that would impact everyone in this university if this did not go well. They told me they understood, as did the others, but they felt that going live was the decision. The executives approved of that, and the date was set. We all prayed for a successful result.

When the data conversion ended, we tested. Everything tested exactly as it should. The cutover was a success. This is a good reminder that if we wait for perfect conditions, we will never move forward.

But before you start running off in the direction of high-risk decisions, let me remind you of the steps the team took before the decision to cut over was made: they had identified risks, took and tested risk-mitigation actions, involved executives and representatives from every department, and devoted hours to prayer. When the decision was made to go ahead, all hands were on deck and all eyes were on the finish line.

Most important, God got major credit, but it was shared with the team who were the much-deserving heroes of the conversion. Their skill, determination, and bravery were rewarded with promotions and generous bonuses.

The team members maximized each individual's skills, stayed committed through many trials, never lost faith in themselves, never lost sight of the objective they were working toward, and communicated honestly to all involved. They were a team that worked. You can have that same kind of team experience.

CHAPTER 3

DIFFERING OPINIONS

I walked into the large ballroom of a hotel for the all-hands meeting of the corporate staff of one of my clients. I was impressed immediately with how festive the event was. Balloon arches stretched over each door. The tables had sprinkled confetti and buttons with positive slogans strewn over them. The stage was covered with balloons and streamers.

As the celebration began, the emcee introduced executives on the stage and acknowledged key individuals in the audience. Then we settled in to view a forty-minute video that chronicled the exciting gathering of all the branch managers, a meeting that had not been scheduled for several years. The video contained much hooting, hollering, costumes, dancing, cheering, skits, marching bands, and big signs flashing commitments to various branch goals.

After the video, the emcee tossed out a few more rah-rah comments and then opened the program to questions from the audience. One brave young woman, whom we shall call Jill, walked up to one of the microphones that had been strategically placed around the ballroom and started speaking.

"It is exciting that all those associated with the branch locations are cheering and talking about a bright future. However, many of us in this room do not know how our current jobs will change or even if we will have them in a couple of months. There are all sorts of plans in process to outsource what we do. It has been stated in more than one meeting that the expectation of the organization is to cut the headquarters' staff in half in a matter of months. I have skills that are in demand and am pretty new to this organization, so I wanted to speak for all those who are scared to say anything because of the retribution that will come their way."

Her voice was very clear, her demeanor was calm, and her message focused and understandable. When she finished, the audience erupted in loud applause, whistles, and cheering.

The face of the usually well-spoken chief executive turned visibly red; his voice became decidedly louder and edgier as he stated, "Do you expect a company to give you a job for life? If you want a job that never changes, you're in the wrong place. We're in a turnaround, and things need to change."

Another executive chimed in that this was the transparency that they had talked about; the fact that the question from the floor was the first time the topic of transparency was addressed did not seem to matter.

Another executive called Jill by the wrong name and discussed the value of change. Jill maintained her composure throughout the entire back-and-forth with applause thundering after every one of her concluding sentences. No one on the stage ever fully recovered.

When the meeting ended and the big ballroom doors opened, the crowd vacated the room like a herd of stampeding animals leaving untouched the tables of fancy food arrangements and yummy-looking desserts. The reaction of the executives became the topic for the rest of the day.

Fast-forward to the next managers' meeting not long after that event. Jill's manager announced that Jill had found another opportunity and would be gone effective the coming Monday. He added that she had solved "our" problem. The chief executive announced that the company would have no more all-hands meetings; it would opt for smaller group gatherings none of which ever occurred.

What a mess. Unfortunately, this mess happens over and over in businesses large and small when the staff disagrees with the management, staff disagrees with other staff, and managers disagree with each other. Silence is the rule for the face-to-face communication, and stabbing is the rule when the meeting ends and all that can be seen is the back side. The result: much unhappiness, low productivity, negative attitudes reflected with customers, and employee engagement headed downhill fast.

Those results are not what any organization wants, and yet I am sure that all of us have experienced some form of conflict in our companies with our managers or other employees. How do we handle it? Leave the company (Jill's choice)? Simply stop communicating with the other party involved? Request the involvement of the human resources department? Silently stew? Or try to get even by winning somehow in another similar conflict?

Mary Parker Follett, a management theorist and early advocate of conflict as a constructive and creative means of problem solving, described conflict as difference. That simplicity brings home the reason that conflict is inevitable. We are all individuals with different backgrounds, races, religions, preferences, skills, mannerisms, educations, and experiences. Our differences are built in from the beginning. Knowing that conflict is inevitable, Follet had this to say about how we should handle it.

> As conflict—difference—is here in the world, as we cannot avoid it, we should, I think, use it. Instead of condemning it, we should set it to work for us. Why not? Know when to try to eliminate friction and when to try to capitalize it, when to see what work we can make it do.[22]

We're never going to get rid of conflict, but we can be prepared to handle it constructively when it comes. When managed appropriately, conflict can serve as a catalyst for change, a path to creativity, and an opportunity for personal and organizational growth.

Methods of Resolving Conflict

How are organizations and groups resolving these inevitable conflicts? Is there one right way? Are they just shoving them under the rug? Though multiple methods exist for resolving conflict, we will focus on three major ones: control and command, compromise, and collaboration. All three are usually needed at some point during the resolution process.

Control and command obviously has one side winning and the other side losing. This is by far the quickest and easiest way to deal with conflict, but it is not likely to be an effective method for all conflicts or for the long term.

Compromise is the way we settle most of our conflicts. In fact, we often see compromise as the goal of dispute resolutions. However, compromising means giving up something of value to each party until everyone arrives at an approved-upon point. No one wins, and no one loses. Many times, all parties walk away unsatisfied because they had to give up items they considered important.

Collaboration is the third way of ending controversy. Collaboration considers the opinions and concerns of all parties. The solutions are usually creative, future oriented, and a combination of many ideas. Compromise deals with what is on the table whereas collaboration creates something new, an innovative solution.

To clarify this approach to conflict resolutions, let me describe a collaborative solution a former client came up with. This large health care organization faced the problem of employees who wanted different or additional days off for the holidays they celebrated—Hanukkah, Chinese New Year, Good Friday, etc. The issue escalated to the point that some employees were going to quit over it, others wanted to explore unionization, and still others thought they had a case for discrimination. Arguing over holidays was getting them nowhere. Collaborative solution to the rescue! Rather than argue about which holidays to include, the hospital eliminated all holidays and gave all employees ten days to use however they wanted. This is the ultimate goal we're looking for. A resolution in which everyone is satisfied.

Before we get into the details of the actual process by which we can manage conflict, let's take a look at how conflict was handled in biblical times to give us a better sense of how Jesus managed it.

Conflict Resolution in Biblical Days

Jesus was no stranger to conflict. He regularly came into conflict with some of the religious leaders of His day and specifically the Sadducees and Pharisees. The Sadducees were wealthy, powerful Jewish aristocrats who did not believe in angels, demons, heaven, hell, or resurrection. In our day, the Sadducees would be considered old money. The Pharisees acknowledged all the doctrinal areas the Sadducees did not. They also emphasized the observance of the legalistic minutiae of the law and were concerned about recognition and honor. The Pharisees would be new money.

There was no love lost between the Sadducees and the Pharisees, but they did have a common enemy: Jesus. On more than one occasion, they tried to get Jesus arrested, killed, and even stoned to death.

Jesus was no shrinking violet in this conflict; He condemned the religious leaders in very clear terms on several occasions and publicly. In Matthew 23:27, Jesus called the religious leaders and teachers "whitewashed tombs, which look beautiful on the outside but on the inside are full of the bones of the dead and everything unclean." A few verses before that, Jesus called the religious leaders "blind guides" and "blind fools" (vv. 16–17). The conflict between Jesus and the religious leaders escalated to the point that they strategized to have Him crucified (see Luke 23:13–18).

John Stott summarized this conflict.

> Jesus Christ ... engaged in controversy. Much of Christ's public speaking took the form of debates

with the contemporary Palestinian leaders of religion. They did not agree with him, and he did not agree with them.[23]

These conflicts and their escalation were all steps in God's plan that led to the cross where Jesus died for our sins. This was resolved with command and control.

God does not like compromise. This goes way back to the Ten Commandments He gave Moses for the Israelites recorded on two stone tablets held in the ark of the covenant and reported in the book of Exodus. God made it abundantly clear in those commandments that "you shall have no other gods before me" (Exodus 20:3). God went on to say, "You shall not bow down to them or worship them; for I, the LORD your God, am a jealous God" (Exodus 20:5). God is not a God of compromise.

He is, however, a God of collaboration. Jesus illustrated collaboration when He had conflict in His team of apostles. In Luke 9:46–48, we read that the apostles were arguing about which of them would be the greatest. Jesus went the inventive, collaborative route and had a little child stand by Him. "Whoever welcomes this little child in my name welcomes me," He told them. "And whoever welcomes me welcomes the one who sent me. For it is the one who is least among you all who is the greatest." He totally turned the tables on them.

Jesus went on to demonstrate the idea of the least being the greatest (today's term is *servant leadership*) at the Last Supper when He took on the servant's job of washing the apostles' feet (see John 13:1–17).

Jesus provided excellent examples for handling conflict: Do not avoid conflict, use it. Do not ever compromise your values to resolve a conflict. Be creative in finding a solution.

Let's look at some current initiatives for conflict resolution that build on the path Jesus laid out.

Safe Environment for Expressing Different Opinions

An environment that will make conflict work for the organization and reap the benefits of creativity and growth must do more than give lip service to the old, tired open-door policy. Management must extend a continual invitation and reminder to express ideas that are contrary to those in the rubber-stamp file. They must prove it is safe to express alternatives to the status quo.

Executives and managers must also be alert to situations and decisions that will clearly not be acceptable to everyone involved and take positive steps toward addressing contrary opinions.

Invite Differing Opinions

Leaders must intentionally work to invite the expression of ideas that differ from those being presented or thought to be the accepted practice. If we just keep doing what we have always done and never look into other approaches or encourage ideas that counter what we have expressed, we will be lulled into accepting the status quo, always coloring within the lines, and eventually becoming irrelevant. Not a future any of us wants. Reminds me of a sign I had on my office wall: "But we have always done it this way."

Inviting differing opinions does not mean we should engage in argument just for the sake of argument, nor does it mean we should condone destructive conflict such as harassment or hostility. It means that we should appreciate and encourage the differing opinions of individuals and groups and discourage what Jack Welch called "superficial congeniality" in a comment on the corporate culture when he first took over as CEO of General Electric.

> I had a strong prejudice against most of the headquarters' staff. I felt they practiced what could be called "superficial congeniality"—pleasant on the

surface with distrust and savagery roiling beneath it. The phrase seems to sum up how bureaucrats typically behave, smiling in front of you but always looking for a "gotcha" behind your back.[24]

Every idea that differs from the prevailing direction does not have to result in conflict. I once presented to those in a department meeting that the next social event would be a potluck picnic in the park next door to our building. Someone in the group piped up with a different idea—have the picnic catered by the spouse of one of our department members. My reaction and that of others in attendance was, "What a super idea!" That was what we did to great reviews.

There will always be efforts to stifle ideas that do not go along with the majority. Do not let that happen. Actively encourage new ideas, and always give them a positive reception. As Sy, Barbara, and Daryl Landau, three experts in the field of workplace conflict resolution, state,

> Too often words like *teamwork* and *consensus* have been misused as a way to stifle divergent viewpoints. An employee who argues strongly for his or her opinion may be accused of not being a team player. That culture will inhibit creative thought. Contention needs to be seen as necessary—as fun![25]

While seeing contention as fun may take practice, research has shown that dissent brings value to the decision process even if it is wrong. "Even when wrong, dissent does two things," says Charlan Nemeth.

> It breaks the blind following of the majority. People think more independently when consensus is challenged. Perhaps more importantly ... dissent stimulates thought that is more divergent

and less biased. Dissent motivates us to seek more information and to consider more alternatives than we would otherwise, spurring us to contemplate the cons as well as the pros of various positions.[26]

I would always tell my staff that if I ever presented an idea or direction that they thought was misguided, was based on bad assumptions, or was simply wrong, they'd better tell me right then and there; otherwise, I would take it higher in the organization, and that group would poke holes in it, and I would not be a happy camper because I'd know my own team had failed me.

Anticipate the Rejection of Ideas

In our opening illustration, Jill, the speaker from the audience, rejected the basic ideas of how the company was doing and the joy of celebration, and the audience members supported that rejection by their cheers and applause. This reaction completely threw the executives for a loop. Why? Earlier that week, they had announced they were outsourcing two departments and aimed to reduce the staff at the corporate headquarters by 50 percent. Could they not have anticipated that some of the attendees might not feel like walking under balloon arches and watching a rah-rah video? Those on the stage seemed so proud of themselves and the meetings with the branch managers that they completely missed that "anticipate" step.

We must never expect initial total agreement when putting forward an idea, direction, proposal, or thought to a group of people. Do not wait to be shot down by someone in the meeting. Anticipate what ideas, areas, or directions might be rejected, and have responses you can quickly and confidently give.

Jesus certainly experienced and expected rejection during His days on earth. He was even rejected by His hometown crowd in Nazareth as He was speaking in the synagogue.

Jesus left there and went to his hometown, accompanied by his disciples. When the Sabbath came, he began to teach in the synagogue, and many who heard him were amazed.

"Where did this man get these things?" they asked. "What's this wisdom that has been given him? What are these remarkable miracles he is performing? Isn't this the carpenter? Isn't this Mary's son and the brother of James, Joseph, Judas and Simon? Aren't his sisters here with us?" And they took offense at him.

Jesus said to them, "A prophet is not without honor except in his own town, among his relatives and in his own home." He could not do any miracles there, except lay his hands on a few sick people and heal them. He was amazed at their lack of faith. (Mark 6:1–6)

The rejection bothered Jesus: "He was amazed at their lack of faith." But it also did not surprise Him. He knew that many would reject His life and message, and He had a ready answer for His hometown neighbors: "A prophet is not without honor except in his own town."

Note that this rejection curtailed the works Jesus could do in Nazareth, so He moved on to teach in the surrounding villages (v. 6). A resolution of conflict might result in needing to adjust the plan and schedule, which changes we should appropriately note and recognize in the regular progress reporting.

Now we have invited and anticipated opinions different from the norms. We cannot ignore the opinions, hope they go away, or just tell those involved to solve it and move on. What do we do?

Manage the Resolution Process

Companies handle conflict in different ways. One of my clients had a large cabin in a wooded area that was used solely for conflict resolution. When a team I was leading had differing opinions on a project issue, off we went to the cabin in the woods, which was staffed by resolution specialists.

We had an initial session with the experts, where they presented their process, so we knew what to expect. We then spent three full days talking, yelling as loud as we could, talking, sitting together in silence, talking, hammering nails into boards, talking, pounding punching bags, talking, etc. At the end of the third day, I think any one of us would have been willing to just flip a coin. But we'd resolved the conflict.

Note that conflict does not mean we argue over whether a meeting should start at 9:00 a.m. or 10:00 a.m. but deals with something significant such as whether the branch offices should be included in a rollout of a new application or whether it should just be the headquarters. Also note that organizations all handle conflict differently and in a variety of ways. It can be a simple office meeting with the parties involved, or it can be comprehensive such as the way we handled it in the cabin in the woods.

The one common thread is the *process* used—whether in a simple or elaborate manner, the following steps should be included.

Present the Areas of Dissention and the Process for Resolution

Clearly lay out the issues and problems that need to be resolved. How do we get from point A to point B? We have more than one way to take that journey, and we want to look at every reasonable alternative. State that this will be a transparent process with all reasonable paths to a resolution sincerely considered.

Then present the process you will follow giving a sense of confidence that you are not going to ignore the conflict and that you are taking it seriously. As the Landaus state, "Until the parties begin to trust each other, they need a secure process they can trust."[27]

This discussion lays the groundwork for everything to follow. Make the objectives of the process clear, spell out the steps and timing, establish the ground rules, and discuss confidentiality expectations.

Rather than using the terminology of issues and conflict, move the focus to *problems* that need to be solved. This approach lessens the attention paid to individuals and their differing opinions and begins to bring all options forward to solve the problems.

Make abundantly clear that if everyone cannot reach an agreement within either an imposed or reasonable time frame, the leader will make the decision. This is a very important point to make. The conflict resolution process is not easy and requires commitment and courage, so do not let the members totally dismiss it by claiming it was just a front of cooperation when the leader was going to make the decision anyway.

Identify the Resolution Team

You may want the entire team involved, you may want a subset of that team, you may want to bring in someone trained in conflict resolution to assist in the process, or you might include staff from other departments who have skills needed for the problem being heard. There is no right or wrong way to put the team together.

The key to the team successfully functioning whatever its ultimate composition is to develop an environment that they can describe by the following terms: *trust, respect, dignity, open, honest, communicative, authentic,* and *prepared.*

That last one is very important—be prepared. Read the material in advance, talk to people regarding any questions, consult others in the organization who might provide additional insight into areas that are not the focus of your professional expertise, and document issues you may want to raise with the team members. It is annoying for a member to waste the entire team's time by asking questions that have already been answered in material distributed in advance.

Which reminds me of my time serving on a nonprofit board. Packages of material were sent to each member well in advance of the meeting giving them all plenty of time to review the material, which included detailed financial information. It never failed as the monthly meeting progressed that some member would ask how we had done the previous month on the money side.

Understand the Dissention

It is important that you understand every aspect of the dissent. What people have expressed is often just the tip of the iceberg or is a summary statement for the many problems that need to be independently identified. You can best accomplish this understanding when you ...

Ask questions. Questioning is a powerful tool for learning. It shows sincere interest and can build rapport and trust, and it demonstrates that the questioner is not a know-it-all but is interested in fully understanding the issue and digging deeper into the reasons for dissention.

Francesca Gino, professor and award-winning expert on the psychology of organizations, comments on the hesitance to ask questions.

We ask too few questions when approaching problems. We work to finish assigned tasks without questioning the process or asking about overall goals. And, rather than celebrating curiosity, our leaders often discourage it.[28]

- Ask honest questions. Use the right words and tone. A question should be a true question, not an accusation. "Why are you always on the other side?" is a question, but the tone and content put it in the accusation bucket. Keep your tone casual and not overly formal or penetrating.

- Ask open-ended questions. Questions that someone cannot answer with a simple yes or no generate more discussion. A question that is always good near the end is, "What do you wish I had asked but didn't?"
- Ask follow-up questions. Solicit more information from the previous answer. This sends the message that you listened, are interested, and want to know more.

In quoting from an interview with former General Electric staff member Donald E. Kane, Richard Pascale stressed that questions are either not asked or are lightly pursued in our quest for answers.

> "Answers" are what we worship. Look at the popularity of TV shows and games such as *Jeopardy*, *Wheel of Fortune*, and *Trivial Pursuit*. "Getting-the-answers" is a national pastime. This makes it very hard for us to live with the questions for very long. We're impatient, want closure, and so we frequently solve the symptoms and not the problem.[29]

Actively listen. Listen to the individual or group with full attention. Ask questions. Take notes. Many times, these same people have been ignored (perhaps to avoid the conflict) and just feel that no one is listening and no one understands what they see as another point of view or option.

In *The 7 Habits of Highly Successful People*, Steven R. Covey offered a succinct statement on understanding in habit 5 in what he identifies as contributing to the success of individuals: "Seek first to understand, then to be understood."[30]

Engage in one-on-one meetings. One-on-one interviews can often be more effective in getting to the underlying causes of dissenting opinions. Some people are not comfortable speaking in a group. The individual being interviewed is also less likely to be influenced by colleagues in the group. As Jack Welch admitted, "'Superficial congeniality' made candor extremely difficult to come by."[31]

If people are to feel comfortable expressing their ideas and problems in the interview, they must trust that you will use their comments appropriately and anonymously. Be honest with them about the degree of confidentiality associated with the conversation.

Narrow the Alternatives

The team now needs to narrow the alternative ways to reach the solution to the problem. Everything is on the table but needs to be condensed into a fewer number of options. Make sure to give special attention to parts of one alternative combined with parts of another: "Dissent also promotes better problem-solving by stimulating the usage of multiple strategies or routes to solutions."[32]

Control Emotions

The "must" in managing conflict is to control the following emotions that are most common in a conflict setting: anger, rejection, and retribution. People may often use these emotions to deliberately intimidate and consequently stifle contrary opinions. You are the only one who can manage this crucial step—Take control of your emotions. Here are some tips to get you started.

Alleviate anger: The Bible recounts several occasions when Jesus seemed angry. Here's a well-known example.

> It was nearly time for the Jewish Passover celebration, so Jesus went to Jerusalem. In the Temple area He saw merchants selling cattle, sheep, and doves for sacrifices; he also saw dealers at tables exchanging

foreign money. Jesus made a whip from some ropes and chased them all out of the Temple. He drove out the sheep and cattle, scattered the money changers' coins over the floor, and turned over their tables. Then, going over to the people who sold doves, he told them, "Get these things out of here. Stop turning my Father's house into a marketplace!" (John 2:13–16 NLT)

We often think of anger as a destructive emotion that we should banish from our set of reactions. It's true that anger can be destructive and even pursued to the point of becoming sinful. However, seeing Jesus become angry at various times tells us that anger itself is not a sinful emotion. What is the difference?

Be angry for the right reasons. Always direct your anger toward the behavior, result, or process, not the individual or the act of disagreeing. Stay on message. Do not drag out stray ideas or actions from the past that are aimed solely at discrediting the individual and the opinion.

Jesus was angry at how the people were dishonoring God and how the temple was being used: "turning my Father's house into a marketplace!" He was targeting sinful behavior, not someone who had disagreed with Him, dared to speak up and challenge His thinking, or disrupted His perfectly planned meeting.

Control your anger. Letting your anger get out of control reflects on you as being a weak and ineffective leader. If you cannot control your anger, how do you expect to control and lead an organization, project, or people?

Jesus was never out of control. The temple leaders did not like what He did, but they could pin nothing sinful or unlawful on Him. Jesus did not let His anger control Him; He remained in control of Himself.

A simple approach that will give you time to control the anger that might be on the rise is to thank the person for expressing that different point of view. You have now recognized the person, acknowledged the opinion, and defused the initial impact. The next steps should be expressed directly and concisely. You might ask the individual to schedule a meeting to further discuss the suggested direction or simply state that the opinion will be on the agenda for the next meeting. What is crucial is that you and the group members do not shut down a valid but dissenting opinion.

Do not stay angry. The leader needs to acknowledge the differing opinion, state in general terms the follow-up that he or she will pursue, and get back to the agenda and objectives. Immediately after brandishing a whip to clear out the temple, Jesus was healing the blind and lame at that same temple, and children were shouting, "Hosanna to the Son of David" in the temple courts (Matthew 21:14–16).

Avoid retribution. By holding a grudge and plotting how to get revenge, you are focusing on the past, wasting mental cycles on ideas for getting even, showing that person who is really the boss, or saving face from what was an embarrassing moment. Retribution is not a topic the Bible puts up for debate.

Vengeance is Mine, and retribution. (Deuteronomy 32:35 NASB)

Do not say, "I will repay evil"; wait for the LORD, and He will save you. (Proverbs 20:22 NASB)

"Never take your own revenge, beloved, but leave room for the wrath of God, for it is written: 'Vengeance is Mine, I will repay,'" says the Lord. (Romans 12:19 NASB)

Make a Decision and Move On

Here is where the leader must step in. Hopefully, you will have found at least one alternative that stands out from the rest. If not, the leader will make the decision.

This will come as no surprise because you discussed the process and timeline at the beginning and continually showed the progress toward the decision date to the team. The leader has listened to everyone and actively participated in the discussion, so the team usually accepts the ultimate decision.

The conflict has been resolved, so move forward. You have clear goals and objectives—results expected, benefits achieved, changes planned, customers better served—Get back to them.

Jesus and His disciples did not let dissention stop them or looked back and wondered if they had done the right thing. They moved on focusing their attention and actions on the mission for which they had been called.

Three's a Charm

Managing teams for a large consulting company presented me with an opportunity to see all three conflict resolution methods in play. One of our best young consultants who was working on one of my out-of-state projects scheduled a meeting with me without any subject for the meeting being mentioned.

Jake (I've changed his name) came into my office at the scheduled time, sat, and said, "Do you know why I married my wife?"

Certainly did not see that coming. "Because you love her?"

"That's true," he said. "And because of that, I want to spend more time with her. If I don't get a local client, I'm going to resign from the company."

Wow—command and control hitting me right between my eyes. When I receive ultimatums like that, I usually show whoever gave them the door and wish them well. But Jake and I had talked often about his family, community involvement, church obligations, and his wife's position at a financial network. Remember that he was one of our best young consultants and had done exemplary work for our clients. I did not want to lose him. I wanted to find a mutually beneficial agreement.

The first thing I did was to tell him that I understood the problem and would find him a local assignment. I said that I could not immediately remove him from the out-of-state assignment. I asked him to give me time to find a replacement, get that person up to speed on the assignment, and then do an orderly transition. He asked how long that would be, and I told him that I would start work on it immediately. I said that I could not give him an absolute date but would certainly keep him in the loop. He agreed with that approach. Whew ... Compromise worked.

I did find a replacement who was excited to get a remote-site assignment, and we were able to pull off a rapid turnover. But this situation gave me the opportunity to raise the out-of-town issue with my colleagues, a problem all of us were increasingly facing as we brought in younger consultants who were actively involved with their families, volunteering in various roles, and being hands on with their children's sports and school activities.

After many false starts, we came up with a schedule that had the consultants work on client projects from the local office on Mondays and Fridays. They would travel on Tuesday, work at the clients' sites for most of Tuesday and all Wednesday and Thursday, and get home on Thursday night. That resulted in only two nights in a hotel. The consultants liked the idea and appreciated that we understood their hesitancy to travel. We piloted the idea on two clients. Everyone was satisfied that the work was getting done, the teams were productive, and conference calls were more than adequate for getting together between on-site days. We very successfully implemented the new plan. Collaboration found an innovative solution.

CHAPTER 4

MANAGING TIME

I attended a time management seminar once in which all the participants had to categorize how they spent their time during the work week. The categories included job related, spouse, general family, and recreation.

After the exercise, we shared our results. One executive listed an unbelievable amount of time devoted to his spouse. The workshop leader asked how he managed to spend that much time with her.

"I sleep with her eight hours every night."

We all chuckled as the leader replied, "Sleeping with your spouse doesn't count."

He fired back, "It would certainly count if I didn't."

It is no wonder we have problems managing our time when it is difficult to even categorize its use. Unfortunately, this is not a recent problem or one resulting from our being always on. This time management challenge dates back to the days of Jesus when Seneca, a Roman philosopher, wrote an essay to his father-in-law responding to the complaint that life was too short.

> It's not that we have a short time to live, but that we waste much of it. Life is long enough, and a sufficiently generous amount has been given to us for the highest achievements if it were all well invested ... So it is: we are not given a short life but we make it short, and we are not ill-supplied but wasteful of it.[33]

Managing our time has been an issue from the days of Jesus and continues to be a problem even with all of the tracking and tools available to us. To understand why this issue has followed us through the ages, let's look at time itself.

Time is the most valuable resource we have. Everyone is given the same number of hours in a day. We cannot deposit the hours in the bank to use later; money cannot buy or rent extra minutes. Once the day is gone, it is gone forever. Time is nonrenewable and irreplaceable.

God gave us the time, and He challenges us through Paul in his letter to the Ephesians to make the most of it: "Be very careful, then, how you live—not as unwise but as wise, making the most of every opportunity" (Ephesians 5:15–17).

Before we put one dollar into major projects or portfolios, we look at available research and perform elaborate calculations to determine what we call return on investment. What will we gain from our invested dollar?

Yet we give very little thought to the return on time before we plunge into an activity requesting our participation. What will we gain from our invested time? Let's answer that question by looking at tasks that will improve the management of our time and increase our return on that investment.

Time Management Task 1: Ask God for Guidance

God has given us every single minute, and He has a plan for using that time. We need to ask for His support throughout the day as we follow His course. Consider how Paul talked about God's purpose for us: "We are his workmanship, created in Christ Jesus for good works, which God prepared beforehand, that we should walk in them" (Ephesians 2:10 ESV). We need to ask God for guidance each morning and then throughout the day as we follow the steps He has laid out for us.

Lloyd Ogilvie, former chaplain of the United States Senate, has a great prayer as you seek the will of God.

> Make this a productive day in which I live with confidence that You will guide my thinking, unravel my difficulties, and empower my decisions. I am ready for this day, Lord, and I intend to live it with freedom and joy.[34]

Time Management Task 2: Write Down Objectives and Activities

Assuming that the mission, vision, goals, purpose, and similar planning elements are in place, it's time to enter the Nike "Just do it!" stage.

The objectives should be key targets that will be the focus of that day's activities. Having a clear objective is another idea that is not new. The Old Testament tells us how David wanted to build a temple in Jerusalem to honor God (see 1 Chronicles 22). He identified the location and started the ball rolling by declaring his objective: "From now on, this is the site for the worship of GOD; this is the place for Israel's Altar of Burnt Offering" (v. 1 MSG).

A current example of an objective, one much simpler than building a temple, is "Email memo to managers regarding the holidays that will be recognized for the next calendar year."

Once you have the objective, write down all the activities you will need to do in prioritized order to accomplish it. This list becomes your plan. Continuing with the temple example, God liked the location but told David that he would not be the builder because he had "shed much blood and … fought many wars" (v. 8). God told David that his son, Solomon, would build the temple (vv. 9–10).

David accepted the decision but thought that his son might be a bit young and inexperienced to erect such an elaborate structure, so David did the planning: "Then David gave his son Solomon the plans for building the Temple" (1 Chronicles 28:11 ERV). And what elaborate plans they were: structure layouts for the entire temple complex, courtyard designs, personnel organization, exact specifications for the gold and silver to be used, and cherub designs (see 1 Chronicles 28:11–18 ERV). David reminded Solomon that these plans were really God's plans: "Here are the blueprints for the whole project as GOD gave me to understand it" (1 Chronicles 28:19 MSG). David then turned the actual building over to Solomon and his team saying, "So get moving—build the sacred house of worship to GOD!" (1 Chronicles 22:19 MSG).

Going back to the current example about the email on the holidays, activities might include: "Obtain final approval on the calendar from human resources," "Review email list of managers and modify as appropriate," "Write, edit, and finalize memo to be emailed," and "Send memo to managers."

It is important to write down what you want to accomplish. Don't get hung up on the format, the appropriate template, or whether to mark them complete with an *X* or a check mark. (Yes, that happens.)

The documented objectives and planned activities give you tools to measure progress throughout the day and reduce the likelihood that you will come to the end of the day with the same activities to be completed as you had when you arrived at work that morning.

Time Management Task 3: Manage Intrusive Interactions

We now have our objective(s) and the actions needed in prioritized order. We arrive at work ready to conquer mountains, and then reality sets in—Our calendar is crowded with interactions that have gotten to be more routine time wasters than worthwhile steps toward our targets. Let's look at the three types of interactions we will encounter: meetings, emails, and reports.

Meetings

Meetings constitute some of the most egregious wastes of time imaginable. University of North Carolina's Professor Steven Rogelberg notes,

> Meetings consume massive amounts of individual and organizational time, with a recent estimate suggesting there are fifty-five million meetings a day in the United States alone. The costs of this meeting time are staggering ... Furthermore, this tremendous time investment yields only modest returns. "Too many meetings" was the number one time-waster at the office, cited by 47 percent of 3,164 workers in a study conducted by Salary.com focused on workplace time drains.[35]

Eliminating all meetings is not an option because they provide valuable communication and interactions. But the effectiveness of meetings can certainly be improved in a number of ways.

Evaluate your meetings and the attendees. List the details of all the meetings you have regularly scheduled on your calendar. Look carefully at each meeting starting with the ones scheduled by another individual or office. Ask yourself these questions.

- Do I really need to be there?
- Could I send a subordinate?
- Could I simply provide input from the distributed agenda?

If you decide that you do not need to be at a meeting (that someone else has scheduled) in person, you need to respond that you are very interested in the focus of the meeting but feel that the person you will be sending has the detail needed for the agenda items, and depending on the agenda items, you will document input rather than attend.

Then check the meetings *you* have scheduled and ask yourself the following questions,

- Do I need this meeting, or are there other means of communication I can use?
- Are all the invitees for this meeting necessary? (Generally speaking, the more people, the less effective the meeting.)

For those meetings you determine are not necessary, send a notice to the invitation list that states you have decided the information exchanged at this meeting could be more effectively conveyed via another method of communication. Then either identify that method or state that you will be getting back to them with the details of that communication method.

When it comes to attendees who are not really necessary, tread lightly. You don't want to unintentionally hurt or anger those you do not invite to a meeting. You can send out a note with the agenda attached stating that you realize their time is valuable and that this meeting might not need their physical presence. Then stress that their input is absolutely necessary and that you would appreciate hearing about anything that they can contribute based on the agenda.

Have a decision agenda. Instead of only listing items to be discussed, include the decisions that need to be made. When those invited see the decision agenda, they will want to have a say in what is decided and hopefully even come prepared.

If no decisions are made, no results are documented, and no resulting actions taken (other than more meetings to further discuss the issues), that meeting was a waste of time. If exchanging information is all that happens, the meeting can be reduced to an informative email.

Shorten the meeting time. Many of us are familiar with Parkinson's Law: "Work expands to fill the time available for its completion."[36] Give the work less time for expansion. Shorten the meeting time. Instead of an hour, how about thirty or forty-five minutes as a starting point?

Manage each meeting. We need to manage to the agenda. Most of us just show up and start down the agenda items hoping the meeting ends sooner than expected. We need to manage the time, the participation, and the decisions. When someone wants to be heard on a subject or disagrees with a decision, listen carefully but do not give up your gavel. If this discussion has surfaced other relevant concerns, suggest another meeting to handle the issues and note that for the minutes. If you are dealing with people who want to ramble on about issues unique to them, suggest that they set up a time to meet with you to continue the discussion. If someone is not participating or is busily staring at his phone under the table, ask him a relevant question. Stay alert. This is your meeting; manage it.

Distribute minutes of the meeting. Document the results and decisions that came from that meeting. If appropriate, make sure the distribution list includes those to whom you report. The simple act of making decisions the focus of the agenda and knowing the bigger boss is receiving the minutes will have a surprising impact on the meeting and the level of urgency experienced.

Emails

Electronic devices have greatly enhanced our ability to communicate. We have emails, texts, emojis, invitations, imbedded speech and music, links, and interesting "sentences" that consist of letters, numbers, and symbols. All are valuable communication tools but are often misused. Consider a few ways we can avoid the abuse of emails.

Electronic communications substituting for face-to-face meetings. Unintended emotions can come across in emails and texts, which means that unintended anger and animosity can build about something. In-person meetings allow us to observe the reactions, tone of voice, and expressions of the person or persons being addressed. Face-to-face meetings are better for building relationships.

Multiple communications required to solve a simple problem. Have you ever tried to find a time for lunch? You can always check the shared calendars, but then you may discover that one or more of the invited do not keep their calendars updated. On and on it goes. Before you attempt to find the location for this lunch, pick up the phone.

Copies. Why in the world does everyone on a team or in a department need to be copied on every email that goes between two managers, two departments, or another entity? If some people are not key to the results expected from an electronic communication, do not include them on the copy line. And I won't even start on the blind copy line!

Reports

Most of the time, the reports that hit your desk or inbox represent not only information overload but also information in the wrong format (e.g., three graphs could possibly have relayed the story now presented in thirty-six pages of single-spaced lines and numbers). You feel responsible to look at the reports and try to understand the meaning and contribute the information from your area that goes into the reports.

As we did with meetings, we should evaluate the reports that come our way and put together a thoughtful document discussing which reports could be eliminated or changed to better support management.

Time Management Task 4: Stay Focused

Focus is very important when it comes to managing our time. Our minds tend to wander, and distractions easily take us on detours that inhibit or delay our ability to achieve our objectives. Let's explore the most common ways to lose or delay focus on our targets.

Being Indecisive

Not making a decision is usually caused by two major feelings: being afraid that something better may come along (fear of missing out has its own acronym: FOMO), and being fearful of making the wrong decision and experiencing failure. Minor hesitation can be positive, but continued indecision wastes time, creates confusion, and stops progress toward objective achievement.

The Bible is not positive on indecision. The apostle James referred to indecisiveness as doubt.

> When you ask, you must believe and not doubt, because the one who doubts is like a wave of the sea, blown and tossed by the wind ... Such a person is double-minded and unstable in all they do. (James 1:6, 8)

On the other hand, we see many positive biblical references on making decisions. David was very decisive when he knew where God wanted the temple built. Jesus was also decisive when He told the fishermen, who had fished all night and caught nothing, to "throw your net on the right side of the boat and you will find some" (John 21:6). And who can forget the decision Jesus made on the cross concerning the repentant thief? "Truly I tell you, today you will be with me in paradise" (Luke 23:43).

How many times have projects or other actions gone off track because no one would step up and make a decision? Decision making is not to be taken lightly, but it needs to be done and done in a timely manner.

Questioning Decisions That Have Been Made

It is difficult enough to make a decision, but constantly wondering if you made the right decision or if you should have chosen an alternative is not productive and potentially weakens your ability to implement your decision. Consider Jesus's opinion about questioning a decision: "No one who puts a hand to the plow and looks back is fit for service in the kingdom of God" (Luke 9:62).

Aviation pioneer Amelia Earhart had a good perspective on decision making: "The most difficult thing is the decision to act, the rest is merely tenacity."[37]

Lack of Persistence

The meaning of "persistent" is "continuing to do something in a determined way even when facing difficulties or opposition"[38]

In his final days on earth, the apostle Paul wrote to a young pastor named Timothy, who was like a son to him. The letter contained instructions to Timothy including this determined charge: "Be diligent [persistent] to present yourself approved to God, a worker who does not need to be ashamed, rightly dividing the word of truth" (2 Timothy 2:15 NKJV).

These are great instructions for all of us—be persistent in doing things that move us toward our objectives. When the day becomes overwhelming and the tasks daunting, all we need to remember is to put one foot in front of the other and move forward. Don't give up. Persistence is accomplished one step at a time. As author Liane Cordes once wrote, "Continuous effort—not strength or intelligence—is the key to unlocking our potential."[39]

No Routines

For many, the mere thought of "routine" can be viewed negatively—looking at anything repetitive as boring. But routines that employ specific procedures for accomplishing specific repetitive objectives can be very helpful when it comes to getting out of the house in the morning, retiring to bed at night, getting ready for the next day, and setting out the clothes you intend to wear the night before. Athletes are known for routines before they bat, attempt a free throw, or kick for an after-touchdown point. Those routines prepare them mentally for the challenges they face. Our routines can do the same thing.

Routines eliminate unnecessary decision making, reduce the risk of forgetting to do something essential, and minimize annoying distractions. Just drop into the groove!

Procrastination

Procrastination is the thief of time. Noted English preacher Charles H. Spurgeon certainly agreed with that statement: "Tomorrow, tomorrow, tomorrow! Alas, tomorrow never comes! It is in no calendar except the almanac of fools."[40] Look at the following negative outcomes from procrastinating and determine to quit putting off actions and start getting things done.

It robs us of opportunities. When Jesus said, "Follow me," to Peter and Andrew as they were fishing in the Sea of Galilee, they immediately left their nets and followed Him (Matthew 4:19–20). On the contrary, we never see in the Bible that those who made one excuse after the other for not following Jesus got another opportunity to do so (see Luke 9:59–62).

No one is guaranteed a tomorrow as so aptly put by the evangelist Billy Graham in his sermon at the Washington National Cathedral two days after the disastrous attacks in New York on September 11, 2001.

> This event reminds us of the brevity and the uncertainty of life. We never know when we too will be called into eternity. I doubt if even one of those people who got on those planes, or walked into the World Trade Center or the Pentagon last Tuesday morning thought it would be the last day of their lives. It didn't occur to them. And that's why each of

us needs to face our own spiritual need and commit ourselves to God and His will now.[41]

It fills us with regret. This point is clearly and sadly made in the poem "Around the Corner" by Charles Hanson Towne.

Around the corner I have a friend,
In this great city that has no end;
Yet days go by, and weeks rush on,
And before I know it, a year is gone.
And I never see my old friend's face,
For life is a swift and terrible race.
He knows I like him just as well
As in the days when I rang his bell
And he rang mine. We were younger then,
And now we are busy tired men:
Tired with playing a foolish game,
Tired with trying to make a name.
"Tomorrow," I say, "I will call on Jim,
Just to show that I'm thinking of him."
But tomorrow comes—and tomorrow goes,
And the distances between us grows and grows.
Around the corner!—yet miles away ...
"Here's a telegram, sir ..."
"Jim died today."
And that's what we get, and deserve in the end:
Around the corner, a vanished friend.[42]

It keeps us from important results. Procrastination does not result in success. It is very easy to let all the deadlines, tasks, problems, concerns, and worries combine to immobilize our actions and prohibit accomplishments. Remember to take that first step and then the one after. James Gordon Gilkey aptly illustrates the "take one step at a time" concept with this metaphor.

What is the true picture of your life? Imagine that there is an hourglass on your desk. Connecting the bowl at the top with the bowl at the bottom is a tube so thin that only one grain of sand can pass through it at a time.

That is the true picture of your life, even on a super-busy day. The crowded hours come to you always one moment at a time. That is the only way they can come. The day may bring many tasks, many problems, strains, but invariably they come in single file.[43]

Time Management Task 5: Just Say No

When a friend asks us to be on a committee, talk to a group, participate on a panel discussion, volunteer as a greeter at a conference, or any other number of requests, we are usually inclined to accept. When someone at work requests our participation in a tour of a recent acquisition, to mentor a new employee, or to speak to interns, we are again inclined to accept. The result is that we end up taking on tasks that invariably take way more time than anticipated and crowd out the work we must complete to accomplish our objectives. When someone requests an activity of you, ask yourself these questions.

- Does this activity need to be done at all?
- Could someone else take on that activity just as effectively?
- Would I be taking it because I am flattered to be asked?
- Is this one of those "urgent" requests that take me away from accomplishing my important objectives?
- Does it have a high, positive impact on me, my department, the organization?
- Does it require a considerable amount of time to prepare and participate?
- Am I saying yes because I want to be liked and will feel guilty if I refuse?

Depending on your answers to those questions, your response may be a simple but polite no.

Seneca had this to say about giving away our time.

> You will find no one willing to share out his money; but to how many does each of us divide up his life! People are frugal in guarding their personal property; but as soon as it comes to squandering time they are most wasteful of the one thing in which it is right to be stingy.[44]

Clear That Account

Imagine you had an account that the bank credits with $86,400 at the start of each day. At the end of each day, the bank deletes what is left in the account. Nothing is carried over to the next day. What would you do? You would make sure to draw out every cent every day. Each of us has that account—it's called *time*. Every morning, God credits that account with 86,400 seconds, and every night, He writes off what has not been used. Time is more valuable than money—Draw out every second of every day.

The writer of Hebrews used the word *today* three times in his short chapter 3. If that word is that important, it is certainly worth your focus as you work diligently throughout the day to clear out the time account. Listen to the words of Solomon: "Keep your eyes straight ahead; ignore all sideshow distractions. Watch your step, and the road will stretch out smooth before you" (Proverbs 4:25–26 MSG).

CHAPTER 5

MAKING DECISIONS

The chief executive officer of my client in the pharmaceutical industry issued the following memo to the entire staff.

> This company cannot attain the objectives set forth nor the financial goals established without making decisions and moving forward with them. If we as a company continue to wait for consensus before anything happens, we are always starting with the lowest common denominator—not a good spot for moving forward. If we wait for the illusive "someone else" to make the decision, we will improve our waiting skills but never move forward. If we continue to ask for more information and aim for "perfect information," the analysis will never be complete, and we will not move forward!
>
> If our leaders insist on being involved in every decision at every level, we will not develop our employees and we will not move forward!
>
> Decision making is critical to forward movement, momentum, and goal achievement! We must improve!

The CEO was right. In my many years of working as a consultant, I've discovered one thing about almost every organization: decision making is a problem. Making decisions is crucial to the success of any leader and any organization. Decision making cannot be avoided or shoved aside. You must make decisions small and large to be successful in your position and to guide the organization to future operational and financial success.

We've discussed decision making in previous chapters more specifically as it relates to those chapters' issues. In this chapter, we will look at decision making as an issue itself. To get us started, let's consider one of the many decisions Jesus made during His time on earth and see how we can apply it to our decision-making skills.

Jesus Decided to Feed the Followers

Jesus was teaching many things to many people in an area near the Sea of Galilee.[45] When it got quite late, the disciples suggested that Jesus send the crowd of five thousand men to nearby villages to get something to eat. Jesus had a better idea and suggested that the disciples come up with the food. Excuses about why that was not possible and other alternatives quickly came from the disciples. Jesus considered the alternatives and made His decision: "You give them something to eat." Jesus then sent them to see what food was already available within the crowd. Their inventory turned up five loaves of bread and two fish.

Jesus directed the disciples to have the crowd sit in groups of fifty to one hundred. He then gave thanks for the loaves and fish, divided the items, and directed the disciples to distribute the food to the crowd. Everyone had plenty to eat, and the disciples gathered twelve baskets of leftovers.

In this story, Jesus clearly shows us the power of strong decision making and how it can positively affect the outcome of a situation. Once He learned of the need, He gathered the information and then acted in a way to solve the need. Strong decisions require discovery, information, and solutions.

The Whole of Decision Making

Finds for Furry Friends (FFF)—not a real company—had been in business for a quarter of a century producing accessories and toys for discriminating pets. The company was very successful, and partly because of that, it had gotten a bit behind in the technical aspects of recent pet products. They hired Charlie, a young, energetic marketing manager whose job it was to update the existing line and find new products that would excite existing buyers and potential parents of fur babies.

Not long after Charlie started, he presented the unique idea of a food bowl that lit up and played music when the pet approached. The lights would be welcoming, and the music would calm the animal. The bowl would be marketed as the Bulb and Ballad Bowl. Charlie needed an approval decision before he could get started producing this bowl.

People are often hesitant to jump into something new, but if they see a process that steps them through answers to their concerns, they will be more apt to climb on board. Fortunately, FFF had a decision-making process in place that Charlie used. Let's watch how Charlie's decision proceeded through the process once again including examples from the feeding of the followers.

Step 1: Understand the Problem or Opportunity

Jesus clearly understood the problem: the people were hungry (see Mark 6:36). He had been dealing with other problems throughout the day healing and teaching, but hunger was now front and center.

Since Charlie knew the Bulb and Ballad Bowl could have a very positive impact on the future of the organization, he decided to take it to the top level of decision makers—the board of directors. He explained to them that the bowl would be the first step in revitalizing the product line and most important boosting their falling revenues.

The discussions regarding the proposed bowl were spirited with the board members stressing that the underlying reason to move forward was to create a more competitive product line. They ultimately approved the proposal, documented that in the meeting minutes, and gave Charlie the okay to move to the second step in the decision process.

Charlie can teach us that we should not proceed until we have a clear, documented understanding of the problem, objective, or decision we need to make. We must be specific in our definition. To help us have that understanding, here are some practical tips.

Avoid dealing with the symptoms. Charlie could have proposed a symptom by merely adding popular colors to the product line. This might have spiffed up some items, but the tired, outdated product line would still be the real problem. It is always tempting to deal with the symptoms and avoid the problems. Handling symptoms is usually a much easier decision to make and one that more than likely has a straightforward approach and can be quickly executed. But fixing the symptoms produces only short-term results and still leaves the decision on the table.

Watch out for the tip of the iceberg. The decision in front of you might be just the beginning of what leads to a large, expensive project. An example of this would be a proposal to update the lobby of an older hotel. Once that is done, the rooms will look shabby. If you try to address the tip of that iceberg by updating the rooms, the bathrooms will look old ... And on and on it goes. Some people call this buying the Jeep by the parts meaning the Jeep is too expensive in total but each part comes under the budget amount so is easy to purchase. The tip always looks affordable, but look beyond and beneath to make sure the iceberg is what you want to tackle. Charlie's bowl could have been the tip of the iceberg if the board did not look at it as the first step in changing the product line.

Step 2: Identify the Decision Maker

Jesus was the obvious decision maker in feeding the five thousand. The disciples tried to influence Him with their opinions, but none thought he had the authority to make a decision about the actual feeding of the masses. Jesus gladly accepted that responsibility and made a decision that required a miracle.

What level or department of the organization originated the issue that needs a decision? Start there to identify the decision maker. If the identified decision maker is reluctant to be in that role, have him or her choose a colleague who would be an appropriate decision maker. Avoid letting the higher-ups gleefully jump into the void. This takes valuable time from the executives, who should be deciding on issues at their level. It also eliminates a teaching moment for the more junior individuals who need coaching on decision making and accepting responsibility.

For Charlie and his bowl, the board of directors continued to be the decision makers.

Check out these practical tips for identifying the decision maker.

Delegate. Delegate. Delegate. What a great opportunity to build the decision and leadership skills of those below you on the organizational ladder. Trusting someone to act on your behalf tells that person that you believe he or she is competent and committed. Remember that you are delegating, not abdicating. Follow up, and be ready to jump in to support the person you have chosen to carry the load of a decision.

Decision makers need multiple inputs. All the board of directors were involved in the Bulb and Ballad Bowl decision. Get opinions from other departments to look at the varied angles of the issue. Make it clear that the decision still rests with the board but that varied opinions would be beneficial in making that decision.

Step 3: Understand the Options and Risks

Jesus listened to those who expressed the risk involved or had other opinions about what should be done. The disciples told Him, "This is a remote place," "It's already very late," "Send the people away so that they can go to the surrounding countryside and villages and buy themselves something to eat" (Mark 6:35–36).

After listening and understanding the risks and options, Jesus made His decision and stated, "You give them something to eat" (v. 37).

That clear decision did not stop the disciples from continuing their appeals: "That would take more than half a year's wages! Are we to go and spend that much on bread and give it to them to eat?" (v. 37).

Jesus heard them once again but did not ask for additional information or suggest that someone else become involved. He stuck to His decision and announced that the first step in implementing that decision was to find what resources were available. He moved ahead and started where He was. He considered options and then made a decision. We need to do the same.

The importance of looking at different views is stressed by Charlan Nemeth.

> Good decision-making, at its heart, is *divergent* thinking. When we think divergently, we think in multiple directions, seek information and consider facts on all sides of the issue, and think about the cons as well as the pros. Bad decision-making is the reverse. Thinking *convergently,* we focus more narrowly, usually in one direction. We seek information and consider facts that support an initial preference. We tend not to consider the cons of the position, nor do we look at alternative ways of interpreting the facts.[46]

Be open to new ideas. If you believe you're the only one who has the answers, the risks are greater in your decision making. You have eliminated the possibility that others may come up with creative ways to solve the problem. As Proverbs 18:15 (MSG) tells us, "Wise men and women are always learning, always listening for fresh insights."

What may come from this step is a hybrid of original thinking, good ideas from options presented, and even a new approach to certain elements. Nemeth sees great value in exploring diverse options.

> When exposed to a dissenting opinion, we think more divergently than we would on our own. We do this whether the dissent is right or wrong. To use a metaphor, we explore different routes. We seek information on all sides of the issue. We explore more diverse options. As a result, we are better able to make good decisions and detect novel solutions.[47]

This is exactly what happened for Charlie. The board of directors asked him to present his proposal to a group consisting of the vice presidents in charge of the major departments. The discussion after Charlie's presentation was not positive. The estimated costs for production were too high to support the loss-leading introductory price they needed to entice the market. No one agreed on the color of the bowl or the lights, and they were a long way from deciding what music the bowl should play. One member of the group just thought the whole idea was dumb. It looked as if the bowl was headed for rejection.

Then someone mentioned running the idea through a focus group of pet parents to see what they thought. Someone else suggested an internal study to determine the lowest possible production costs. Bingo! They put together their concerns and questions for the outside agency that would conduct the focus group. They would hear from two focus groups implementing the suggested changes from the first group prior to conducting the second focus group. Running parallel with the focus groups, an internal study by representatives from the procurement and manufacturing departments would investigate ways to lower production costs.

Make sure you are honest on the risks that could hinder project progression, gather as much information as you can realistically obtain (you will never have it all), and seriously consider the options and new approaches you've heard others articulate. Then make a decision.

Here are some practical tips on understanding the options and risks.

Do not consider any decision an either/or at the outset. Draw out options or disagreements through questions, what ifs, similar solutions, and competitors' actions. Encourage creative ideas. Mary Parker Follett warns that decision makers can be "bullied" by the either/or approach.

> Our outlook is narrowed, our activity is restricted, our chances of business success largely diminished when our thinking is constrained within the limits of what has been called an either-or situation. We should never allow ourselves to be bullied by an "either-or." There is often the possibility of something better than either of two given alternatives.[48]

Do not swallow the vendor's pitch. It probably seems unnecessary even to mention this point, but I have seen it happen too many times. Even when research raises all sorts of red flags, the decision maker will still jump at the opportunity to implement this perfect solution.

A large business client of mine was considering replacing a computer application that was key to its operation. Every customer used this application. It reported revenue, needed to operate in 2,500 locations, and was essential for meeting strict regulations for the industry. The current application performed well but was too old to utilize new technology.

A vendor had gotten the ear of the CEO, so all the decision makers were invited to the product demonstration, which showed the product to be a perfect fit (of course). Subsequent research unearthed facts such as that the company had been in business for only eight years, had only six small-scale customers, had a staff of eight, and would not release financial data. Despite the many red flags, the CEO signed on the dotted line to implement the system. The implementation was a disaster. The only positive aspect saving the company from a total meltdown was that the system failed miserably very early in its implementation, so pulling back and starting over was not a widespread embarrassment.

Do not be intimidated by higher-level executives. Executives sometimes have a preconceived idea about what the decision should be and will wonder why those on the decision-making team don't just go with that decision and get on with life. Those executives can come off as intimidating. This is the time when you need to refer to the process and summarize where you are and the next step you need to take. This lessens the personal aspect and stresses the neutral process. Award-winner researcher Francesca Gino refers to this issue.

> Power aggravates the problem. As we climb the organizational ladder, our ego inflates, and we tend to feel even more threatened by information that proves us wrong. If we're not careful, being in charge can, over time, close us off to what others have to offer.[49]

Step 4: Make a Decision

Jesus made a clear decision: "You give them something to eat." He knew He was the one to make the decision. He had listened to other opinions and options; He knew the risks. Now comes the main point: make a decision!

Back to Charlie and the bowl. The results came back showing that the focus groups liked the bowl idea. They also provided the input needed for the colors and suggested a simple instrumental number for the music. Better yet, the internal team discovered a manufacturing plant that already produced simple bowls and could add the required lights and music for a small incremental cost greatly reducing the estimated production costs. Everyone was on board. The revised details moved the board of directors to the positive decision of moving ahead with the production as the first action in updating the entire product line.

The key to decision making is to choose what you think is the right thing to do and do it. Do not delay, do not toss it to someone else, do not involve those who should not be involved, do not abdicate your responsibility to someone else; step up and make a decision—the one you think is the right one. Make sure your decision is communicated to the organization and then implement your decision decisively. Follow Jesus's advice and let your yes be yes (see Matthew 5:37). Take responsibility for that decision.

Do not question or rethink your decision. Decisions are hard enough to make, so do not continue to make the same decision. Bringing uncertainty into the mix is confusing to the implementation team.

Do not underestimate intuition. Intuition is based on many been-theres-and-done-thats. Those gut feelings come because something in your memory triggers them. Value your experiences and the intuition stored in your memory bank because of the many times you have faced problems, issues, blocks, missteps, and successes. Don't overplay your hand in this situation; remember that intuition is not a mystical vapor but the result of many learning situations.

Step 5: Follow Through

Jesus made sure He did everything He could to make that decision successful. He determined the seating arrangement, He used His disciples as the waiters, and He had His disciples clean up afterward gathering twelve basketfuls of broken pieces of bread and fish. Then He moved on to His next miracle: walking on water.

Charlie orchestrated the follow-up for the bowl. The production department stayed on top of producing them. The sales department blanketed the market with advertising and made personal calls to the distributors. Finance was tracking the bottom line for any early alerts that might be helpful. The bowl was on its way to being a successful new item.

You need to follow up on your decisions making sure that all is being done the way it is supposed to be done. Clear the way for operational success, make sure others are making progress, and clean up the little pieces left over. Maybe parts of the decision implementation might not be working. Admit that. Tackle the alternative direction and again move forward. Here are some practical tips for following through.

Track back with involved employees. If the implementation required training internal employees, talk to those people to see how they are doing. Now that they have actually been applying what they were taught, they may have questions or even improvements you can make.

Correct problems that have occurred. You're bound to encounter problems as you move forward with the decision. Listen to those who express issues and concerns, jointly decide on solutions, implement those solutions, and keep moving.

Simple Sells

A potential vendor demonstrated a simple decision approach to my client in the transportation industry. The organization was in the market for a new system to handle its cargo operations. I was serving as an advisor to the process and to the decision committee, which comprised executives, department managers, and employees who would use the system daily.

The market scan for available systems turned up three that would meet the basic needs. Our committee invited each of the three vendors to spend a day on site with the management and staff to understand what the current system did and the desired functionality of the future system. Then each vendor team presented its product and how it met the needs of my client.

In the first two presentations, the vendor teams gave glowing technical displays that showed their products to be the best on the market and certainly ones that satisfied my client's present and future requirements. The third vendor walked up by himself and presented several slides all with the same format and no technical enhancements. The format was a grid with four columns headed Functionality, Yes, No, and Required Changes. Each of the present and desired functions was listed down the left of the page with either a check under Yes that the systems had it or No followed by the changes that would be required to give the system the desired functionality. He took questions, thanked everyone, and left.

That vendor's presentation was black and white, simple, and effective. We knew exactly how that system would perform in our environment and knew in advance what modifications would be necessary to give us our dream system. He had built a level of trust.

The evaluations were fairly close, but my client went with the vendor who gave the simple presentation. They felt they knew what they were getting.

The simpler the decision-making process, the more straightforward the results, and usually the stronger the decision—*and* the more successful it is. A simple approach serves you and your decision making well.

CHAPTER 6

PERFORMANCE REVIEWS

The Bible contains performance reviews from Genesis to Revelation. In Genesis 1, God evaluated His own performance during each of the first five days of creation: "God saw that it was good" (vv. 12, 18, 21, 25). At the end of the sixth day, God summed up His performance, which included the creation of Adam and Eve: "God saw all that he had made, and it was very good" (v. 31). In Revelation 2–3, Jesus evaluated each of seven churches and offered encouragement for what they were doing right and criticism in areas where they were failing along with corrective action. Between the first and last books of the Bible, we can find many such performance reviews, examples of God defining responsibilities and the accountability expected.

Fast-forward to today. Performance reviews can be sources of exasperation, and many sink to the level of useless. Some of my clients have simply eliminated them. On the opposite side, a few clients have invested heavily in employee performance and promotion linking career goals to reviews and educational opportunities. One client considered performance reviews equal in importance to the budget. Consequently, the management team at that client devoted many days to reviewing employees, discussing results within departments and across the organization, comparing employees in like positions, and arriving at the scores, promotions, salary changes, and education plans. Not surprisingly, that client had an exceptionally high-performing staff.

As much as we may dread performance reviews, they have value. Rather than eliminating them out of frustration, we need to figure out how to integrate them into our businesses in a way that leverages their benefits and avoids the many personal and legal pitfalls that frequently accompany their use.

As we consider how to best follow and use performance reviews, let's consider the performance evaluation model we find throughout the Bible, which includes three key steps: start right (hiring process or onboarding), succeed continually (evaluating and coaching), and stop professionally (terminating process or offboarding).

Let's take a closer look at each step. For each step, I've included a key result we need to keep in mind and pursue to minimize confusion we may encounter because of the independent and legally demanded extra steps that often find their ways into reviews. Keep your eyes on each objective as you traverse the many demands of performance management.

Step 1: Start Right

Key Desired Result: Employee knows the role and expectations of the position and is confident of the organization's support.

Jesus provided a great example of starting off on the right foot with new employees when we heard what He told those called to be His disciples. Let's look in as Jesus called the brothers, Peter and Andrew.

> As Jesus was walking beside the Sea of Galilee, he saw two brothers, Simon called Peter and his brother Andrew. They were casting a net into the lake, for they were fishermen. "Come, follow me," Jesus said, "and I will send you out to fish for people." At once they left their nets and followed him. (Matthew 4:18–20)

Jesus made sure that the brothers knew what was expected of them: "Follow me" and "fish for people." Though they had much to learn about that assignment, they knew what they were to do and were convinced that this was the path they wanted to follow. They also trusted Jesus to give them support, teach them the skills they needed, and guide them as they fished for people. The call to Peter and Andrew shows us how to take that first step in assuring all new employees that they have made the right choice in joining our organization. Here are other ways to do that.

Discuss the Company History and Current Goals and Objectives

A good starting point is to share with new employees the company's history as well as its goals and objectives. This will bring the new employees up to date and make sure they understand the big picture—where the company is going, how it intends to get there, and what overall purpose the company wants to accomplish. If appropriate, give them a tour of the facility.

Provide Each Employee with a Current Organization Chart

New employees will understandably be unsure of how the organization works and who reports to whom. To help get them up to speed, provide them with an organizational chart. Circle the spot in the organization that shows their position, those above them, those below, and colleagues. This chart also implies promotion paths and easily leads to the next step.

Clearly State the Role(s) and Responsibilities

As with Peter and Andrew, new employees want the onboarding process to state the role(s) and responsibilities they will be assuming and how they fit into the larger picture of the company. When the company's goals are not reflected in the goals of the individual, a McKinsey study found the following to be a typical ground-level reaction: "Managers think we aren't sophisticated enough to connect the dots, but it's obvious when our goals get disconnected from what really matters to the company."[50]

Stress Accountability

Each person is responsible for achieving the agreed-upon goals and objectives. The manager should always stress that the employee should schedule a meeting with him or her if it looks like existing conditions will hinder goal accomplishment. Individual accountability transitions nicely to the assessment process.

Provide Assessment Process Information and Forms

Give each employee a copy of the performance assessment process and forms. Now they are fully aware of the way, frequency, and involvement of others in assessing how they have accomplished their objectives as well as ideas for improvement and further education.

Make Introductions and Follow Up

Introduce the employees to their managers or supervisors. The managers or supervisors should take it from there. A great foundation has been laid for the new employees.

The managers or supervisors can follow up and build on that great foundation by reiterating the employees' roles and responsibilities, showing them their work spaces, making sure they know the work hours, introducing them to others in the department, ensuring the technology they require is set up, and answering any questions they have.

Onboarding is just the beginning of the help provided to new employees. You'll want to allow for frequent follow-up to provide the direction and assurance they need to keep them on the track to success.

Jesus provided an example of this continual help as He allowed His apostles to follow Him in learning the skills necessary to move from tradesmen to fishers of men. John MacArthur describes Jesus's training throughout this period.

> The Lord Himself stuck closely with them. He was like a mother eagle, watching the eaglets as they began to fly. They were always checking back with Him, reporting on how things were going.[51]

Step 2: Succeed Continually

Jesus had no backup plan; the disciples *had* to succeed. His training plan included three essential components, which we look at here.

Check Progress Consistently

Key Desired Result: Employee is on track with performance objectives.

As we noted in Luke 9:10, Jesus kept a close eye on His apostles and expected progress reports: "When the apostles returned, they reported to Jesus what they had done. Then he took them with him and they withdrew by themselves to a town called Bethsaida." Jesus listened to their progress and took them aside to discuss those reports.

The first essential component to helping employees succeed continually is checking their progress consistently. This step involves actually evaluating them and through that evaluation process assuring each person that you care about her or him and the career path chosen in the company.

Each manager must meet personally with all individuals who report directly to her or him. Managers need these people. Make sure that you are all moving in the same direction to accomplish the same goals.

How often this meeting occurs depends on the evaluation cycle and how the employee is performing. Give this meeting your entire attention.

Feedback should be two dimensional and fair. Two dimensional means that both the manager and the employee are respected and heard. But what is fair? The McKinsey study wrestled with this question and fell back on a tight definition from the academic world.

> Procedural fairness [is] ... the practical question of whether employees *perceive* that central elements of performance management are designed well and function fairly. This eye-of-the-beholder aspect is critical. Our survey research showed that 60 percent of respondents who perceived the performance-management system as fair also stated that it was effective.[52]

Span the term of the evaluation. It is not fair to evaluate only on the most recent activity, which is foremost in your memory. Make notes regarding the employee's performance throughout the entire evaluation period.

Link employee goals with company goals. As we stated previously, this is a very important point. If the company goals have changed, work with the employee to adjust his or her goals.

Be direct. Make sure that the employee understands everything you are discussing with him or her. Neither of you should leave the meeting wondering what went on.

Be specific. Do not refer to "all" or "many" but refer to specific instances where that employee's actions have been less or greater than expected. Refer to the notes you have been taking.

Suggest improvements. No one is perfect. Making solid suggestions indicates once again that you care about the employee and her or his success in the company.

Be very clear on next steps. Action items should come out of this evaluation, and all of them should be referenced in the employee's next evaluation.

Ask for feedback. Ask and then listen. Graciously receive feedback on your actions without getting defensive. This will instill a confidence in the employee that he or she is a valued part of the team and that you are interested in his or her success.

You might be surprised at the feedback on your own performance. A client engaged my team to conduct what is called a 360-degree evaluation. This evaluation seeks input from those organizationally above the individual being reviewed, from those organizationally equal, and those organizationally below the individual. This client was experiencing unusually high turnover of employees and was seeking to find the causes of that turnover. Management approved the questions and administered the evaluations. My colleague and I expected comments along the lines of "The person does not give clear directions," "My pay does not reflect the impact that I have made," and "The managers do not pull their full share of the load." We were wrong. The surprising comments were "They never smile," "They go straight to their office and close the door," and "They never call me by my name." Sometimes, letting employees know that you care about them can be as simple as a smile.

Document meeting results. Keep good notes and file them in the appropriate locations.

Coach Effectively

Key Desired Result: Target coaching to individual.

During His earthly time with His disciples, Jesus had many coaching opportunities. One of the most notable was with Peter, a hard-charging, impulsive, hot-tempered fishman when Jesus called him. Because of Jesus's effective coaching, Peter went on to be the rock on which Jesus built His church (see Matthew 16:18).

Let's consider one example of the way Jesus coached. This example is cited in Matthew, Mark, and John always following the miracle of feeding the five thousand, which we have mentioned. The version we'll look at for this example is from Matthew 14:22–34.

At the end of a very busy day, the disciples boarded a ship to cross to the other side of the Sea of Galilee while Jesus stayed behind to pray. By the time Jesus finished, the boat with the disciples was in the midst of the sea being tossed about by the wind and the waves. Jesus decided to get to the boat by walking on the water. When the disciples saw Jesus through the mist, they thought He might have been a ghost. Between the storm and the ghost, they became very fearful. Jesus calmed their fear by calling to them, "Take courage! It is I. Don't be afraid" (v. 27). When Peter saw and heard Jesus, he immediately went into action. "Lord, if it's you," Peter shouted out to Him, "tell me to come to you on the water" (v. 28). Jesus responded, "Come" (v. 29). Peter got out of the boat and started walking on the water. When he saw how rough the wind was, however, he began to sink and called to Jesus for help. "Immediately Jesus reached out his hand and caught him. 'You of little faith,' he said, 'why did you doubt?'" (v. 31).

Note that Jesus did not let Peter sink but reached out His hand to save him—and *then* He offered the advice. That is basic and effective coaching. In all coaching meetings, it is critical for the manager to stress that the objective of the meeting is to personally help the employee. Follow up on criticism with ideas for the employee to get on a better path. Use praise to encourage a higher level of achievement. Put the following into practice.

Ask what help the employee needs. This is often the first step to meaningful coaching. Use your evaluations and daily observations to start the conversation. Just hearing the problem may guide to a solution.

Help the employee discover alternatives. There is never one right way to solve a problem or to arrive at a desired result. All managers and particularly relatively new ones need to be coached in this area. They do not want to be wrong, and they often think their solutions are the only way to go. Warning: do not jump in and take over the issue. Though that may be the easiest and fastest solution, it does nothing to help the employee.

Thank and encourage the employee. How often do we overlook the value of a simple thank-you? Actively look for areas and activities that deserve appreciation and jump in to give it. Write a short, simple note thanking them for something they did. Even when they have not reached the desired goal, encourage them by recognizing their efforts but also remind them that the finish line is still ahead. Show confidence in them. As Boyd Bailey rightly observed, "No one has ever complained about too much encouragement."[53]

Become your team members' advocate. Recognize them to others and in front of others. Never take credit for work they have done—That is demoralizing, has a negative effect on the employees, and reduces any positive impact associated with your coaching or managing.

Coach your best performers. This may seem counterintuitive, but no matter how much energy you put into poor performers, they rarely get to the level of your best performers. Focus on the best performers to produce the results you need. As human resources expert Susan Heathfield notes,

> It is ironic that many managers find that they spend the majority of their time with their troubled, or underperforming employees. This is despite the fact that the most significant value from their time and energy investment most often comes from the opposite priority.[54]

Jesus knew Peter's shortcomings when He first called him to be a disciple, but He saw his potential and prophetically named Peter for what he would become: "Jesus took one look up and said, 'You're John's son, Simon? From now on your name is Cephas' (or Peter, which means 'Rock')" (John 1:42 MSG). Coach for the potential that you see.

Coach those with performance issues. While the greatest return may come from coaching your best performers, those at a lower performance level need to receive the chance to succeed as well.

Regular coaching will cause minor problems to surface before they get to be major distractions.

Peter had many performance issues, and Jesus handled them in various ways. When the soldiers came to arrest Jesus, Peter immediately drew his sword and cut off the right ear of the high priest's servant. Jesus sternly responded, "Put your sword away!" (John 18:10–11). Stern coaching.

All four Gospels tell of Peter's denial of Jesus. The story started at the Last Supper, when Jesus told Peter that "before the rooster crows today, you will deny three times that you know me" (Luke 22:34). When the soldiers led Jesus away to the house of the high priest, Peter followed "at a distance" (Luke 22:54) and then went into a courtyard and sat with others who had gathered by a fire. Three times, people came up to Peter and claimed that he was a follower of Jesus. Three times Peter denied it … Then the rooster crowed. *"The Lord turned and looked straight at Peter.* Then Peter remembered what Jesus had said about Peter's denials and "went out and wept bitterly" (Luke 22:61–62, emphasis added). Coaching with just a look.

Then after Jesus's crucifixion and resurrection, while Peter was back in his boat, he saw Jesus on the shore. Peter did not wait for the boat to dock but jumped into the water and swam to shore. After finishing the breakfast that Jesus prepared for Peter and the others, Jesus reinstated Peter saying once again, "Follow me!" (John 21:19). That's coaching through the failures that will inevitably come and not writing someone off.

As you coach through performance issues, make sure you are on the same page as the employee concerning them. Share examples. Focus on the behavior, not the employee.

Work with the employee to solve the performance problem. If performance continues to be an issue, place the employee on a performance improvement plan (PIP), a formal written plan to provide structured meetings with the employee, provide documented coaching and feedback, and formally measure performance against plan and expectations. If performance continues to be a problem even with the PIP, employment for that employee may be terminated.

Compare Levels of Performance Objectively

Key Desired Result: Differentiate compensation across levels of performance.

Here come the advance warnings. "All the members of my team are terrific. I cannot reward some more than others." "Why make everything so complex? Just use a salary grid—over, down, and done." "Everyone always finds out who is paid what and then everybody is unhappy."

But let's counter those complaints with insights from Bob Briner, a leading figure in sports management, and Ray Pritchard, the president of a noted international preaching ministry.

> Perhaps the first thing to learn about all types of rewards is how important they are. No leader can afford to take them lightly. Wise leaders consider them prayerfully ... Obviously, monetary rewards had little if any part to play in the earthly leadership of Jesus. He rewarded his disciples in other ways—time with him, unique experiences, great teaching ... rich relationships to replace the ones they had lost ... Rewarding those we lead is a very complex leadership responsibility and privilege. Jesus is the best model to go to for guidance.[55]

Rewards are powerful. They can provide tangible gratitude for past actions; they can provide motivation for performing at a high level in the future; or they can be considered unfair, demotivating, and a reason to look for other employment. We want to make sure that we skew the reward to the positive end of its power.

The individual evaluation sessions have been held. Every manager has assigned each member of his or her staff a score. Now it is time to start looking at all the employees across department functions to differentiate according to past actions, future potential, and value to the organization. The first step is to schedule a meeting of all the department managers who report directly to you.

The meeting you call is very important, and a hundred percent attendance should be expected. This is a working meeting to compare employees across department functions and to come up with appropriate compensation. This is where the managers get to tell you about all the things they and their team members have done in their areas and brag about those who have done it. Not all will be rosy, but it is important to continue to build relationships and develop a strong team that can effectively manage the department.

Each direct report should present the evaluations they did on the employees in their department, section, area, or territory. Rank the employees according to the evaluation given by his or her manager.

Your direct reports then rank all the employees at that level. Use A, B, C, D, or 1 through 4. Do not use more than four levels because any further differentiation becomes useless discernment for awarding the compensation by ranking level. There may be some grouped areas for a project team, new employees, etc., but these should be very clear exceptions.

Do not give up. This is not easy, but it is well worth it. Partners in talent and organizational management of McKinsey weighed in on this topic.

> Don't kill ratings. In the quest to take the anxiety
> out of our performance management—especially

when there's a bulge of middle-range performers—
it is tempting to do away with rating systems. Yet
companies that have tried this approach often
struggle to help employees know where they stand,
why their pay is what it is, what would constitute
fair rewards for different levels of performance, and
which guidelines underpin incentive structures.[56]

At least in North America and Western Europe, you need some
form of documented administrative evaluation to make employment
decisions; otherwise, you must treat everyone exactly the same.
Completing this ranking needs to be the major objective of this
meeting. Here is a suggested process.

Focus on the extremes. This includes employees who are not
pulling their weight, are late or absent more than usual, and who are
clearly not working on the same level as others in like positions. They
should not be getting paid the same as those who are contributing
at least an average amount daily.

The employees who are extremely good performers and
recognized as that by their peers should be rewarded accordingly.

Your employees recognize these extremes and will look at that
differentiation in pay as being fair.

Move on to the big middle of the pile. You need to differentiate
even if in broad groups no matter how difficult that is. Look at the
specific objectives and the level of accomplishment, the support of
team members, the going-beyond efforts, the importance of the tasks
assigned, and the willingness to take on tough assignments. Here is
where notetaking throughout the year becomes very important. Also,
collect input from managers outside your area who have worked with
them throughout the year.

Look at improvement steps. What specific steps can the employee
and the manager take to bring the C's up to B's and the B's up to
A's? These steps need to be included in the performance expectations
and reviews.

Identify consequences for not engaging in the performance-improvement activities or simply not improving performance.

Consider intrinsic motivation and nonmonetary rewards. More money is always most welcome, but sometimes, other benefits can be high on employees' want lists. Flexible benefits have become a popular incentive for many employees. Hard not to like limitless vacation time!

Also consider other rewards based on a unique culture: family inclusion on company-planned holiday celebrations, pets allowed at work, fitness center memberships, subsidized meals, childcare, doggy day care, and on-site common services needed such as dry cleaners and post office.

Offer special assignments with high visibility. Allow them to attend special events or conferences. Recognize them in the workplace.

Provide time off for *pro bono* work. One of my clients made each employee list a personal objective for evaluation at the same level of importance as the business objectives and then provided time off for those objectives. This was very popular because it allowed employees time to coach a little league team, volunteer at an animal shelter, serve as president of the parent-teacher organization at the child's school, etc., all with the company's support.

Avoid personal comparisons. Each individual is handled as just that—an individual. He or she is evaluated on his or her performance. That performance should never be compared explicitly to another individual or group member.

When questioned about the rating, the individual should be told why he or she was rated in that category based on specific activities in their objectives.

It is always tempting for employees to want to know how other employees compared to them or how someone else was rated. Don't fall for it. Remember how Jesus handled this temptation. Right after He refocused Peter on his purpose, Peter started asking about John. Jesus gave a very simple answer, "What is that to you? You must follow me" (John 21:22).

Step 3: Stop Professionally

Key Desired Result: Respect the individual.

There are two reasons for stopping the professional relationship between the organization and an employee: termination and resignation.

When an Employee Is Terminated

Termination can come as a result of a number of reasons. Here, we are referring to an employee being terminated for not performing according to expectations. We are not talking specifically about an employee being released as part of a reduction in force. Though many of these points apply to both, our primary focus is on the employee's inability or unwillingness to perform satisfactorily.

As you work through the termination process, you want to do so professionally.

Have all documentation in order. Make sure the documentation is accurate and complete, illustrates negative performance progression, and shows continuous dialog with the employee regarding these performance issues. Without this documentation, any litigation that follows may result in damages to your reputation and finances.

Schedule a face-to-face discussion. Make every effort not to terminate via email, text, voice mail, phone call, or any other not-in-person communication. Have a member from the human resources team involved in this meeting.

Provide date and time of termination to essential other employees. While keeping the employee's termination as confidential as possible, you will need to alert certain individuals in other departments such as the technology department so they can turn off all access to the systems.

Keep your meeting brief. In the meeting, summarize the key performance problems from the documentation. Keep it brief. Do not go into any details, and do not answer questions that usually turn out to be circuitous. Explain that the employee needs to return all company-owned items. Thank him or her for his or her service and end the meeting.

Offer a soft landing when possible. Depending on the company policy, offer the employee a soft landing with a termination package that includes such things as salary and benefits for a specified period, outplacement services, etc.

Set a time for them to come back to clear out their offices. If the employees did not have company-owned items with them at the time of termination, those should be returned on this date. This allows the person dignity in leaving and still allows them to retrieve their personal belongings.

Document the meeting and file in the appropriate locations. You'll need to keep this information in case litigation or other issues arise.

When an Employee Resigns

We also hope that the employee will act professionally in the way he or she resigns. Regardless, as soon as you become aware of the resignation notice, schedule a face-to-face discussion about the decision to take another position either within the company or at another organization.

If appropriate during this discussion, let them know how valuable they have been to the department and how they will be missed.

Schedule a time to meet with them and their manager to discuss knowledge transfer. This is extremely important and should be a discussion that goes to the lowest level possible. Meet with the manager regularly during this process to make sure it is on track.

Wish them the very best in their new position, and again let them know how much you appreciate their contribution.

Document the meeting and file in the appropriate locations.

In both cases—whether terminating or facing a resignation—move on. Do as Jesus did. Jesus had become famous for His ministry and His miracles when He returned to His hometown of Nazareth and started speaking in the synagogue. Everyone spoke well of Him after He spoke and asked, "Isn't this Joseph's son?" (Luke 4:22). Jesus then told them that He knew they wanted Him to perform the same miracles in His ministry as He had done in another area, but He said He was not going to do that. This infuriated the townspeople, and they ultimately got angry enough to try to kill Jesus by throwing Him off a cliff. Jesus "walked right through the crowd and *went on his way*" (Luke 4:30, emphasis added). Maintain your forward motion.

You Are Ranked Very High, But …

My team and I were conducting an audit of the information technology department of a client to find ways of improving what they did and how they did it while still substantially reducing costs. A major part of this audit was to evaluate and make recommendations regarding the organizational structure and the staff.

During this audit, we interviewed Ron (name changed), the auditor for the tech department. He was terrific at what he did and was at the top of the employee ratings. When it came time to talk to him about our recommendations, we accurately reported that he was one of the best employees the company had in this area but that we were going to recommend eliminating his position and obviously his employment in the department. The dramatic cost reductions we were committed to making required that auditing be done in a different manner, and we simply couldn't justify keeping on a dedicated staff member for that function.

Ron was very gracious and asked about other positions for transition. We asked what positions he thought would generate the passion he had for auditing and provide the job satisfaction he deserved. None came to his mind. We were fortunate to be able to provide a reasonable time for him to find something as well as offer him a generous termination package.

Fast-forward a few months when I got a call from Ron, who had found a wonderful opportunity at another company. He could not thank my team enough for their honesty and for forcing him to look for another position. He was making more money and was already up for a promotion. Today, he is at the top of his game, and he and I still communicate.

Though not all situations will have that kind of outcome, you'll want to build all staff evaluations and the subsequent actions on a base of open, honest, and genuine concern for each individual. These evaluations will run the gamut from exciting to one of the most difficult things you will ever do, but the result will strengthen and move your organization and you forward.

CHAPTER 7

MANAGING PROJECTS

How often have you wondered if a building would ever be completed? When the company website would finally move from the Coming Soon phase? Why your own kitchen remodel was weeks late and cost way more than you planned?

Delivering on the promises of projects has been notoriously unsuccessful for decades. Look at these statistics.

- Only 19 percent of organizations deliver successful projects.[57]
- One hundred thousand pounds squandered by the BBC on a video archives system that never materialized.[58]
- Dissatisfaction with project portfolio management increased in the three-year period from 2016 and 2018 by 11 percent to 56 percent.[59]
- Only 34 percent of organizations complete projects on time or on budget. Only 36 percent deliver the full benefits of their projects.[60]

They're dismal!

All sorts of tips and tricks have been added in response to the often-reported negative statistics regarding project success: new project methodologies have been introduced, certifications and the appropriate educational offerings expanded, and organizational structures changed in attempts to address the issues. In spite of the many resources focused on improving project success, the results continue to disappoint.

A major reason managing projects is so difficult is that it brings every problem-area issue we have identified in the preceding chapters together in one bundle. No wonder projects fail. The good news is that it doesn't have to be that way. And Israel's Nehemiah is just the man who can show us how to hone our project management skills to complete successful projects.

Who Is Nehemiah?

In 596 BC, the Babylonians devastated and destroyed Jerusalem. They demolished the temple, broke down the city walls; and burned its gates (see Jeremiah 25:11). Most of the Jews were taken as captives to Babylon. In 539 BC, the Persians conquered Babylon, and Persia's reigning king, Cyrus the Great, decreed that the Jewish captives be allowed to return to Jerusalem (see Ezra 1:1–4).

Many of the Jewish people remained in captivity. A remnant, however, returned to Jerusalem and began rebuilding their lives and their city. As hard as they tried, they could barely make a dent in the reconstruction, so they eventually gave up. Years went by, and Jerusalem remained broken and burned.

Nehemiah, born in captivity, had risen to the trusted position of cupbearer in the palace of King Artaxerxes of Persia. Nehemiah had never been to Jerusalem but had heard stories through the years about its beauty and power. Most important, the residents who had made the long trip to Jerusalem from exile were his people.

When one of Nehemiah's brothers and some others from Judah came to visit, Nehemiah asked how Jerusalem and its current residents were doing (see Nehemiah 1:2). They answered, "Those who survived the exile and are back in the province are in great trouble and disgrace. The wall of Jerusalem is broken down, and its gates have been burned with fire" (Nehemiah 1:3).

The news troubled Nehemiah to the point that he "sat down and wept ... mourned and fasted and prayed" for weeks (Nehemiah 1:4).

Nehemiah then took the courageous step of asking King Artaxerxes if he could take a leave of absence to go to Jerusalem to rebuild the walls (see Nehemiah 1:4–6). This was a big request since Nehemiah would be leaving a very important palace position for an indeterminate time.

Nehemiah's prayers were answered when the king granted the leave and provided him with letters of reference, captains of the army and horsemen for protection, lumber for building the wall, and a home to use while he managed the rebuilding project (see Nehemiah 1:7–8).

Nehemiah overcame obstacles and strong opposition to complete the wall around Jerusalem in a record time of fifty-two days (see Nehemiah 6:14–15).

The Action That Is Paramount to a Project's Success

The one action that was paramount to Nehemiah's success— an action that permeated every phase and every deliverable in his project management—was that he prayed. He prayed for God's guidance, strength, wisdom, words, and much more. Consider the ways he prayed.

Before starting the project. "For some days I mourned and fasted and prayed before the God of heaven" (Nehemiah 1:4).

Before asking the king for support. "The king said to me, 'What is it you want?' Then I prayed to the God of heaven, and I answered the king" (Nehemiah 2:4–5).

When facing ridicule. "Hear us, our God, for we are despised" (Nehemiah 4:4).

When facing fear. "We prayed to our God and posted a guard day and night to meet this threat." (Nehemiah 4:9)

Throughout the project. "Remember me with favor, my God" (Nehemiah 5:19).

When giving thanks and credit at the project's successful end. "On that day they offered great sacrifices, rejoicing because God had given them every joy" (Nehemiah 12:43).

This is something we must do as well if we are to successfully carry out project management tasks. After completing our time of prayer, a time that is continually present throughout the entire project, we are ready to dive into the project phases.

Project Phases

Let's take a deeper look at the steps Nehemiah took, align those steps with the demands of today's business environment, and produce the following project phases: define the business proposal, develop the business plan, drive the results, and declare success. We see these phases illustrated below.

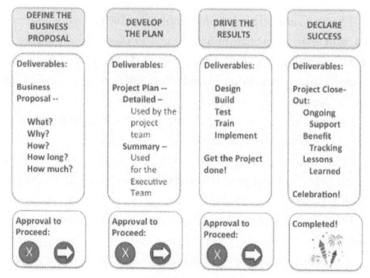

Project Phases

Note that there is a "gate" at the end of each phase. Executives will review the deliverables from each phase to answer the following questions: Is the information as complete as expected for the project at this phase? Is the project still worth pursuing? If the answer to each question is yes, this project will be approved to proceed to the next phase. If not approved, requests for additional information may be made or the project may be terminated.

Now let's turn our attention to the progression of the phases. Because activities may overlap between the four project phases, the actions we discuss throughout the phases can apply to the entire management process. Additionally, repetition from prior chapters may occur because we are bringing all the problematic issues together in this chapter on project management.

Phase 1: Define the Business Proposal

First, you will need to know what the project is. The best way to do this is to define the business proposal. This also is the most important step toward successfully completing a project and achieving its anticipated benefits.

In order to define it, you'll need to answer these five questions.

1. *What* is the project? Here, you are looking for the objective, external entities impacted, and company entities, departments, and key individuals impacted.
2. *Why* should this project be done at this time? You want to consider the risks of doing and not doing as well as the benefits tangible and intangible.
3. *How* is the project objective going to be achieved? Here, you will develop a high-level plan showing activities and associated accomplishments.
4. *How long* will this project take? You'll need to include a timeline with the high-level plan.
5. *How much* is the project going to cost? You'll want to know the bottom line—the total dollar amount.

The answers to all questions will be at a high level because the project is at the idea stage. Since a go/no go decision will be made regarding this project, however, you'll need to take care to provide answers that are as accurate as possible. Do not give answers that guarantee a positive response by being overly optimistic—That approach will come back to bite you as the project progresses and the answers to the questions are continually refined.

Nehemiah answered these questions amazingly well when King Artaxerxes asked, "What is it you want?" "Send me to the city in Judah where my ancestors are buried so that I can rebuild it" (Nehemiah 2:4–5).

Nehemiah went on to set a time; request "letters to the governors of Trans-Euphrates, so that they will provide me safe-conduct until I arrive in Judah," and request physical resources via "a letter to Asaph, keeper of the royal park, so he will give me timber to make beams for the gates of the citadel by the temple and for the city wall and for the residence I will occupy" (Nehemiah 2:6–8).

King Artaxerxes gave Nehemiah the approval to proceed and "sent army officers and cavalry" with him (Nehemiah 2:9).

The project proposal that needs to be presented in today's environment will no doubt require a bit more documentation than was required of Nehemiah. But the one step you cannot skip or minimize is that of taking ownership of the project.

Own the project. Nehemiah was concerned enough about the Jewish remnant who had returned to Jerusalem that he specifically asked his brother and others for a report upon their return from that area. When Nehemiah heard the disturbing report, his concern turned to a commitment to do something for those people. In his subsequent prayer, he identified with the people and their problems. He put himself in their shoes. Nehemiah owned the project (see Nehemiah 1).

A good project manager needs to own the project. The manager must be committed to the objective and benefits, continue to drive the mission, motivate the team members to a high level of productivity, continually sell others on the idea, battle to get the best talent, build the team up when times are tough, keep the executives involved and committed, negotiate successfully when differences arise, and effectively handle conflict inside and outside the project team.

Managing a project is not for the timid or those who want to remain objectively distant. As we will see through Nehemiah's journey, it is an intense effort that requires dedication, commitment, and determination to navigate all the obstacles and arrive at the mission, objectives, and benefits.

Phase 2: Develop the Business Plan

Phase 2 is where the project moves from idea to initiation. The proposal has been approved, and the planning to make the proposal a reality is underway. The five questions, which are key guides throughout the entire project, help build the necessary detail required to actually operate as skilled members of the team, manage the activities, and communicate progress to the executives who are funding the project.

Going forward, there will actually be two plans: a detailed plan—This shares detail to a very low, micro level, which the team can use to identify and track the work on a daily basis; and a summary plan—This summarizes the detailed plan to allow the executive team the opportunity to readily understand it at a glance.

What specific actions should we take during this phase of developing the business plan?

Listen and ask questions. Nehemiah started questioning those who had just returned from Jerusalem: "Hanani, one of my brothers, came from Judah with some other men, and I questioned them about the Jewish remnant that had survived the exile, and also about Jerusalem" (Nehemiah 1:2–3). Notice that Nehemiah listened and questioned. In some of the preceding chapters, I have commented on the importance of questioning while listening. It indicates you are interested and delves into areas you might not have gone into had it not been for the questions asked.

As the manager of a project, you need to ask questions regarding the problems that will be solved with the completion of the project, the expectations for benefits, and the participation of those from the specific departments. Use this opportunity to build relationships with those involved. When things go sideways during the project, these are the people who will jump in to get the project back on track.

"Smart questions make smarter people," writes Frank Sesno in *Ask More*. He continues.

> We learn, connect, observe, and invent through the questions we ask. We push boundaries and we discover secrets. We solve mysteries and we imagine new ways of doing things. We ponder our purpose and we set our sights … Questions—asked the right way, under the right circumstances—can help you achieve both short-term and lifelong goals.[61]

Listening and asking questions are vital to ascertaining and understanding the answers to the key questions of what, why, how, how long, and how much. This is also an essential step you'll need to continue doing in every phase during all the project activities.

Visit the sites involved. After being in Jerusalem three days, Nehemiah "set out during the night" to inspect the walls. He told no one about this inspection and was very careful not to be discovered during the process taking "no mounts with me except the one I was riding on." (Nehemiah 2:11–12). The following map provides details of the city, wall, gates, and inspection.[62]

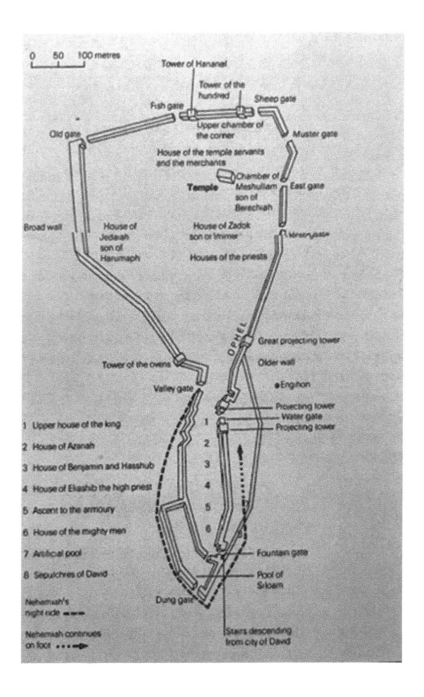

0   50   100 metres

Tower of Hananel

Tower of the hundred

Fish gate

Sheep gate

Old gate

Upper chamber of the corner

Muster gate

House of the temple servants and the merchants

Chamber of Meshullam son of Berechiah

Temple

East gate

Broad wall

House of Jedaiah son of Harumaph

House of Zadok son of Immer

Houses of the priests

Inspection gate

OPHEL

Great projecting tower

Older wall

Tower of the ovens

Enrogel

Valley gate

Projecting tower
Water gate
Projecting tower

1   Upper house of the king   1

2   House of Azariah   2

3   House of Benjamin and Hasshub   3

4   House of Eliashib the high priest   4

5   Ascent to the armoury   5

6   House of the mighty men   6

7   Artificial pool   Fountain gate

8   Sepulchres of David   Pool of Siloam

Nehemiah's night ride ▬ ▬ ▬   Dung gate

Nehemiah continues on foot • • •▶   Stairs descending from city of David

113

Now that all possible preparations had been completed, Nehemiah was ready to meet with the officials and those who would be doing the work. He explained to them, "You see the trouble we are in: Jerusalem lies in ruins, and its gates have been burned with fire. Come, let us rebuild the wall of Jerusalem, and we will no longer be in disgrace" (Nehemiah 2:17). He also gave credit to God and just happened to mention that the king was on his side. Those involved replied: "Let us start rebuilding" (Nehemiah 2:18).

Like Nehemiah, you need to visit the sites involved. Schedule meetings that include tours of production facilities, retail locations, manufacturing plants, transportation hubs, care centers, etc. Take those opportunities to discuss the project, and ask about the impact it will make on those units.

Take and verify notes. Verify everything. Document the notes you take in a digital form and send them to the person you met or the person responsible for getting a group together. Make sure that what you understood is accurate. To avoid having this become a dreadfully time-consuming effort, use a template and stick to information directly related to the project only.

Set up meetings. Connect with people by setting up meetings preferably in person and particularly in the beginning. You'll want to meet with all executives and those reporting one level below the executives who are likely to be involved in the project. Be respectful of the individuals and their time, but ask questions. Discuss everything in inclusive terms—*our* needs that will be filled, *our* problems that will be solved.

Get a clear understanding. Understand any assumptions, basic units, and calculations used for the schedule, costs, and benefits. Different areas have different measures that are tracked and reported. Do not be intimidated by numbers. Often, you will find it helpful to set up a one-on-one with a staff member in the financial area to go over the calculations and the meaning of the varied results that will be used throughout the project.

Get buy-in from all levels of the organization. Nehemiah had official authority from the king to rebuild the walls. He could have marched right into Jerusalem and scheduled the kickoff meeting. Instead, he knew that even with the approval from the top, he needed the cooperation and support of those who would be the team of volunteers. Remember that Nehemiah gathered the facts, studied the overall plan, and validated the project needs in preparation for meeting with the local officials. With all of the details in hand, he clearly articulated the problem and requested that the local officials work *with* him for the solution—to rebuild the walls (see Nehemiah 2:16–17). Nehemiah had support from all levels, and the building could begin.

Formal approval from the top may get the project funded and on the list of approved activities, but it will not assure the support needed to cross the finish line with the checkered flag wildly waving. Make sure to get committed support from all necessary levels. Continue to meet with those who will be involved with or impacted by the project. Build relationships.

Do your homework. Fully understand the project and the needs it will fill, the problems it will solve, the effort it will take, and the impact it will have on all levels of the organization. Remember, you own the project!

Be prepared to negotiate. There may be requests for additions to functions, adjustments to schedule, increased involvement, etc. Listen carefully and consider them all valuable requests. Assess and document the impact of the requests, and review the findings with the one(s) making the requests. It may be that you can incorporate some of the requests, alter them to have less of a negative impact, or add them to the list of functions to be considered for future releases. Then make sure that any changes are thoroughly documented and included in the answers to the five major questions.

Build teams that work. Nehemiah had the workers excited as we see from their statement, "Let us start rebuilding." Now, they must put the statement into action—Saying and doing are two different things. Nehemiah 3:1 records action: they "went to work." There was not a lot of jockeying for the best jobs or arguing over how to get the job done; they simply did what they needed to do.

The following principles will help you keep the project teams on track.

Make sure team members are committed to the mission. Nehemiah 3 records the names of the people who helped to make the wall happen—in less than two months! They were working together (Nehemiah 3:1–2) and were committed to a mission (Nehemiah 2:17–28). If you keep focusing on the mission, the minor issues will be seen for what they are and the progress toward the mission will continue.

Ignore differences. There were priests, men of Jericho, men of Gibeon, goldsmiths, apothecaries, ruler of cities, Levites, merchants, a man with his daughters, and many others involved in the project. Certainly they had differences, but they chose to overcome them for the sake of the common goal (Nehemiah 3).

Disregard the uninvolved. The nobles cited in Nehemiah 3:5 were too important to work on such a plebian task. Their lack of commitment was recorded, and the work went on without a hitch.

Always do what needs to be done. Other nobles (eight different rulers listed in chapter 3) exhibited humility in taking orders instead of their usual giving them. The ruler of Beth-Haccerim even repaired the dung gate (see Nehemiah 3:14). No prima donnas please.

Beware of requested changes. Changes can be common to any project, so you'll want to beware and be aware of any requested changes to any aspect of the project including its scope, objectives, deliverables, schedule, cost, staffing, and benefits. Ask the questions necessary to assess the impact to the organization in general and the specific results and benefits anticipated for the project.

Trust those who are most closely involved. In every phase, listen to those actually doing the work and testing the product. The project team is involved with the project for a significant period resulting in their thorough understanding of the system, product, or service being developed, not so with those seeing and using it for the first time. Listen to all concerns, and discuss these with the project team members responsible. Always close the feedback loop with the user or tester who addressed the issue.

Keep abreast on required ongoing support. As the project nears its completion, ask questions again regarding the ongoing support required as well as the intensive care period when the project first goes into production. The answers first received may have an added element of urgency now that the go-live date is fast approaching.

Give another listening and questioning tour. Once the project is in production and being widely used, go one more round with the listening and question asking. Focus this round on problems that need to be addressed in subsequent releases, expectations versus delivered results, and benefits being realized.

Phase 3: Drive the Results

Methodologies, reporting standards, and communication methods need to be in place, but when we get down to the basics, people make everything happen. It is essential that the project be staffed with individuals who possess the needed skills, have the requisite experience, are committed to the project, and have a positive can-do attitude.

Start recruiting from day one. When you meet with the executives to solicit support, stress the importance of the project to them and ask if they have any ideas for team members in their areas. Once you gain their concurrence for the value of the project, they will want people from their organizational area on the team, which can make it more successful. Without commitment, the executive starts thinking about who would be missed the least.

Keep the mission and the associated benefits constantly in view. When decisions need to be made, when problems arise, when requirements are modified—keep the goal and benefits at the forefront. Always communicate with others the impact on the ultimate mission of the project.

Break each project activity into multiple tasks. The word *section,* meaning "a distinct part or portion of something bigger,"[63] is used over and over in Nehemiah. Just looking at the first eight verses of the third chapter, we see five references to "section" (Nehemiah 3:2, 4–5, 7–8).

When discouragement was setting in, Nehemiah made the decision to finish the entire wall but only at half its height (Nehemiah 4:6). Now, the workers could see the wall, vision it at full height, and regain enthusiasm for the project.

Each of these tasks or sections should be completed in as short a time as possible. Start by asking that no task be longer than an estimated eight hours. This will not be possible, but it will provide guidance regarding what you consider to be short. Establishing minor and major deliverables allows for more-frequent success, which breeds success, excitement, and enthusiasm.

Reward success. Projects are exciting in the beginning and very rewarding at the end. But absolutely necessary is that middle part, which can be filled with hard work, missed deadlines, complaints, and changed requirements. So commit to rewarding success during the entire project but particularly through that difficult middle. That will communicate to everyone that you appreciate their efforts. Here are some simple rewards.

- Say "Thank you." Nehemiah made sure everyone knew that he appreciated all they had done.
- Single out individuals. Everyone likes to be thanked personally. There are seventy-one individuals thanked in Nehemiah 3.
- Be specific. Say thank you for a specific task that they completed. "They laid its beams and put its doors with their bolts and bars in place" (Nehemiah 3:6).

- Acknowledge a great attitude. Single out for appreciation those team members who are always positive and always willing to help. "Baruch son of Zabbai *zealously* repaired another section" (Nehemiah 3:20, emphasis added).
- Show gratitude for extra effort. The person who stayed an extra half-shift to fill in for a late team member or the one who took the new team member under his or her wing—offering a word of thanks is very much appreciated. "Meremoth ... repaired the next section ... [then he] repaired another section" (Nehemiah 3:4, 21).
- Provide physical rewards to the team. Hand out small but useful items when a deliverable date is achieved, give an afternoon off with pay for solving a difficult problem, or provide gift cards for working over a weekend. Be aware that rewards regularly given become expectations and no longer serve to motivate or enhance productivity, so vary the rewards and the reasons.

Value diversity in your team. Diversity means more than differences in culture and ethnicity. It means different backgrounds, experience, education, personalities, and drive. Valuing diversity also means that you need to value and work through dissention. If everyone thinks the same thing, you do not need a team or a project—just put the objective on the to-do list of an individual.

Manage conflict. As stated above, a diverse team will have to work through dissention in the ranks. Each situation is unique in some ways, but the following list presents ideas that you can use consistently to manage and resolve conflict.

- Recognize and manage conflict quickly. Conflict is unavoidable in the workplace, and it will not just go away; it will intensify over time. So you'll need to manage it, not ignore or fear it.

- View conflict as an opportunity. Whenever a disagreement comes up, all involved have the potential for learning and growth. Divergent positions can stimulate innovative solutions.
- Listen carefully. Identify the basic conflict with those involved. Stick to the events and actions. Avoid personalities and emotions. Develop potential solutions.
- Focus on the mission. Keep the main thing in focus— the mission. Do not allow conflicts within the team to negatively impact the accomplishment of the project goals.

Hire an outside consultant only if you do not have the skills available in your organization. Make sure the consultant is considered a valuable team member and participates in appropriate meetings and events. You may grouse a bit about having the consultant anywhere but chained to the desk because of the hourly rate, but having a cohesive team will facilitate knowledge transfer, diverse opinions, and positive results.

Measure and report progress. Being on the job, putting in time, and being a congenial team member are expected but are not the keys to success. Expect, communicate, and reward results. Be honest. Do not deliberately show results to be better than the actual state of completion. This often happens because the person working on that task is sure that he or she will "catch up." The catch-up never happens and the shading of the results can get out of control quickly. When it is discovered, the credibility of the entire team will be questioned.

Manage the opposition. The opposition to rebuilding the wall around Jerusalem started early and escalated throughout the project. It did not take long for the officials of neighboring towns to express their displeasure: "When Sanballat the Horonite and Tobiah the Ammonite official heard about this, they were very much disturbed that someone had come to promote the welfare of the Israelites" (Nehemiah 2:10). The opposition got into full swing with the ridicule. Sanballat started with, "What are those feeble Jews doing? Will they restore their wall? Will they offer sacrifices? Will they finish in a day? Can they bring the stones back to life from those heaps of rubble—burned as they are?" Then Tobiah sarcastically added, "What they are building—even a fox climbing up on it would break down their wall of stones!" (Nehemiah 4:2–3).

Then it escalated to threats of attack: "Before they know it or see us, we will be right there among them and will kill them and put an end to the work" (Nehemiah 4:11).

The attack now became personal. First, they wanted a meeting to negotiate a solution. The meeting was to take place in a dangerous area for Nehemiah. They requested this meeting four times, and each time, Nehemiah responded that he was too busy to make that trip (see Nehemiah 6:1–3). The second attempt was libel, accusing Nehemiah of building the wall so that the Jews could revolt against their king (see Nehemiah 6:5–7).

The final blow was to bring disgrace upon Nehemiah: "Let us meet in the house of God, inside the temple, and let us close the temple doors, because men are coming to kill you—by night they are coming to kill you" (Nehemiah 6:10). Nehemiah would not run away or violate the rules of the temple.

Nehemiah's responses to all of these opposition tactics were to pray for guidance, respond in a direct manner with the truth, prepare for the follow-through on the threat, and keep on working.

Our response to opposition should be the same.

- **Answer the opposition directly, dealing specifically with the statements made.** If possible, directly relate the response to a negative impact on the project, e.g., Nehemiah's response in regard to the meeting request: "I am carrying on a great project and cannot go down" (Nehemiah 6:3) rather than being concerned for personal safety in that area.
- **Pray and prepare.** Nehemiah had a powerful and practical faith: He prayed for safety on his journey to Jerusalem but

also accepted "officers of the army and cavalry" as escorts (Nehemiah 2:9). When the opposition threatened to fight against Jerusalem, Nehemiah prayed and "set up a guard against them day and night" (Nehemiah 4:9). When the threats of force escalated, he reminded the workers that "our God will fight for us" (Nehemiah 4:20). And as he prayed, he continued the rebuilding with half the workforce performing the work while the other half carried weapons in case of attack (Nehemiah 4:16). Take the opposition seriously and prepare direct, accurate responses that focus on the project and its mission.

- **Continue the work.** The best answer to the opposition is to continue toward the mission and goals of the project. There will be compromises that relate to the opposition and compromises internal to the team, but as much as possible, do not allow the opposition to stop the forward momentum of the project. Pursuing the mission and objectives encourages the project team and discourages the opposition. The team needs to know that you are fighting the opposition and moving ahead.

Communicate to be understood. Nehemiah was a powerful communicator: he communicated his vision to King Artaxerxes in such a way that his request to build the walls was approved as well as his request for safe travel and resources (see Nehemiah 2:4–9). He communicated the details of the plan to the city officials with a persuasion that caused them to respond with "Let us start rebuilding" (Nehemiah 2:18).

His communication with the team of workers was very effective. In his book on Nehemiah, Cyril Barber summarized Nehemiah's communication as being "able to coordinate the efforts of the group, ensure cooperation, commend honest effort, see that each task is completed satisfactorily, and provide for open lines of communication between employee and employer."[64]

Communication in all formats and throughout the project life cycle must be easily understood, clear and concise in its statement, and comprehensive enough to support decision making.

Don't have weight requirements for the documentation. Many project management methodologies have evolved to the point of demanding reams of documentation sometimes eliciting comments about tests for weight and thickness. While that may be a bit of an exaggeration, there are too many examples of users not understanding what the project delivered and ending up with a system or product that did not satisfy the needs they had expressed. Make sure the business proposal, requirements, test results, and progress reporting are stated in terms that everyone can easily understand.

A great way of solidifying exactly what a system, product, or service provides is to create a list of every project feature, function, or objective that is important to you. During the various meetings and discussions, be very direct in asking if that requirement is currently met by the system, product, or service. Not *could* it be done or *will* it be in a future release, but *does* it currently fulfill the identified requirement?

Document decisions and issues raised in various meetings. Distribute the documentation to the project leads for verification or correction.

Understand the project progress reports. What are the rules for "on time," "late," "deferred," etc.? This is very important when progress is stated as red, yellow, or green. The colors should have objective guidelines and not be left to the opinion of team members.

Assess impact to the project by any changes to the key questions. When any answer to the key questions of what, why, how, how long, and how much changes, first, clearly understand the change and the reason. Then make sure that the impact on the project is documented in subjective terms and in the objective schedule and dollar tracking.

Know the numbers. We can clearly see Nehemiah's knowledge of numbers in Nehemiah 7:6, where he lists those who were living in Jerusalem.

The whole company numbered 42,360, besides
their 7,337 male and female slaves; and they also
had 245 male and female singers. There were 736
horses, 245 mules, 435 camels and 6,720 donkeys.

Nehemiah continued to number the residents within the tribes
in Nehemiah 11.

There is one consistent language all executives understand: the
language of money. There is no alternative to knowing and fully
understanding all numbers involved in a project. The project team
should include a member of or at least a direct liaison with the
finance department. This team member and the project manager
must march in lockstep throughout the entire life cycle of the project.

You'll also need to understand and report the financial
measurements that the organization uses. What interest rates are
used in calculations? What depreciation method is used? What are
the rules for capital versus expense?

Then keep digging until you can put some actual numbers to
the benefits being claimed. Some benefits have clear dollar values
while others are harder to quantify. "Better" and "more efficient"
are impressive intangible benefits, but it is much stronger to show
"better" as a specific reduction in call-center activity and "more
efficient" as a reduction of one day in the financial closing cycle.

Finally, check and recheck your numbers. Whenever you present
a group of numbers on an exhibit, the people reviewing the exhibit
will recalculate your math and make sure to tell you of any errors.
One error in the numbers and you have reflected on the integrity
of every number being presented. Check, check, and check again!

Phase 4: Declare Success

A project has a beginning *and* an end. Too many projects
just drift into the shadows never to be heard of again. Might be

an interesting *Where Are They Now?* series unearthing projects involving "Six Sigma," "Business Process Reengineering," or "Matrix Management." But you cannot declare success until you've completed the project. So when you do complete it ...

Wave the checkered flag. Nehemiah threw a huge party to celebrate the completion of the wall. The leaders of Judah were on top of the wall, two large choirs marched in opposite directions from the top of the wall, and musical instruments provided the accompaniment. Great sacrifices were offered, and "the sound of rejoicing in Jerusalem could be heard far away" (Nehemiah 12:43).

Maybe you did not accomplish all your objectives. Maybe you did run over budget. Maybe there are unhappy users and grumbling team members. But key objectives have been reached, the project has positive impact, and benefits are being achieved. Projects will never be perfect, but they need to have a purposeful and positive ending.

Prepare and present a final report that clearly states the final objectives that were met and those that were not met. Close out the budget. Compliment the team members' efforts and contributions. Thank the executives for their support. If appropriate, identify future phases or releases and the issues that will be addressed in each.

And celebrate!

Tie the red bow. After celebrating, Nehemiah took care of the everyday tasks that needed to be performed now that the wall was in place: "Men were appointed to be in charge of the storerooms for the contributions, firstfruits and tithes" (Nehemiah 12:44). The musicians needed to be supported so Nehemiah made sure that "all Israel contributed the daily portions for the musicians and the gatekeepers" (Nehemiah 12:47). Nehemiah tied up all the loose ends.

Whatever we do, be it project management or a routine job responsibility, we need to be sure to tie up the loose ends. As a consultant, I was taught an important lesson by Joe Izzo, the founder of the JIA Management Group, the consulting company that was brave enough to take me on as a consultant with no experience. He taught me to tie a red bow.

- Provide performance reviews to the managers of the project team members who will now return to their regular duties.
- Make sure that any incentives promised to project team members are calculated correctly and delivered.
- Organize and store all project documentation.
- Release storage used by the project both digital and physical.
- Clear the company calendar of all project-related dates.
- Monitor the benefit measurement that should be underway making any necessary changes.

As J. Willard Marriott, founder of Marriott Corporation, said, "It's the little things that make the big things possible. Only close attention to the fine details of any operation makes the operation first class."[65] Projects and the participants create unique opportunities. The paths to success will take different twists and turns. The success rates for projects are not good, but you can change that. Follow Nehemiah!

NOW IT IS YOUR TURN

Solving the unsolvable is exciting, challenging, frustrating, and ultimately rewarding. It is my hope that this book has increased your ability to avoid the many traps and embrace the challenging steps to success.

Jesus and others highlighted through the chapters were frustrated and sometimes downright scared, but they never gave up. Nehemiah built the wall despite the vicious attempts by those who opposed it. Jesus persisted in changing a ragtag bunch of apostles into a brave and bold group who changed the world. When it looked like all was lost on Good Friday after Jesus had been crucified, here came Resurrection Sunday. You don't have to give up either.

A positive attitude and a never-give-up determination will go a long way in guiding you through the issues and solutions we've identified together. Let the apostle Paul's words in Philippians 3:15–16 (MSG) be a constant reminder that you can be successful as you move forward in your work.

> Let's keep focused on that goal, those of us who want everything God has for us. If any of you have something else in mind, something less than total commitment, God will clear your blurred vision— you'll see it yet! Now that we're on the right track, let's stay on it.

ACKNOWLEDGMENTS

My sister, Carrie Hanna, who had me and my book on her prayer list for the entire time it took me to complete this. She was always there.

Joe Izzo, the brave company owner who hired me into my first consulting position. He has been in on this book since the beginning, and whenever we would meet, his first question was, "How's the book coming?"

And to the One who never leaves me and sees me through the good and bad times, my Lord and Savior Jesus Christ. This book needed His infusion of wisdom and guidance every time I sat down to write. May any glory and honor be sent His way.

ENDNOTES

1   Peter F. Drucker with Joseph A. Maciariello, *Management*, revised edition (New York: HarperCollins, 2008), 319.

2   Michael Hyatt, *No-Fail Communication* (Franklin, TN: Michael Hyatt & Company, 2020), 15.

3   Drucker, *Management*, 319.

4   Peter F. Drucker with Joseph A. Maciariello, *Management*, revised edition (New York: HarperCollins, 2008), 319.

5   Jack Welch and John A. Byrne, *Jack: Straight from the Gut* (New York: Grand Central, 2001), 393.

6   J. Oswald Dykes, *The Manifesto of the King: An Exposition of the Sermon on the Mount* (London: James Nisbet & Co., 1881).

7   Willy Steiner, "Silence in Communications: 5 Reasons Why Silence Makes You a More Powerful Communicator," Executive Coaching Concepts, January 23, 2018, https://executivecoachingconcepts.com/silence-in-communication/.

8   Kare Anderson, "Who Packs Your Parachute?" *Forbes*, November 18, 2015, https://www.forbes.com/sites/kareanderson/2015/11/18/who-packs-your-parachute/?sh=1a9720ab717d.

9   Drucker, *Management*, 319.

10 C. Gene Wilkes, *Jesus on Leadership: Timeless Wisdom on Servant Leadership* (Carol Stream, IL: Tyndale, 1998), 212.

11 Alexander Balmain Bruce, *Training of the Twelve: Passages Out of the Gospels, Exhibiting the Twelve Disciples of Jesus Under Discipline for the Apostleship* (Edinburgh: T. & T. Clark, 1871), 30.

12 Tim Hansel, *Eating Problems for Breakfast: A Simple, Creative Approach to Solving Any Problem* (Nashville: Word, 1988), 194–95.

[13] John MacArthur, *Twelve Ordinary Men: How the Master Shaped His Disciples for Greatness and What He Wants to Do with You* (Nashville: Thomas Nelson, 2002), xiii.

[14] Bruce, *Training of the Twelve*, 30.

[15] MacArthur, *Twelve Ordinary Men*, 26.

[16] Ibid., 38.

[17] Boyd Bailey, *Learning to Lead Like Jesus* (Eugene, OR: Harvest House, 2018), 176.

[18] Welch, *Jack: Straight from the Gut*, 332.

[19] David A. Kravitz and Barbara Martin, "Ringelmann Rediscovered: The Original Article," *Journal of Personality and Social Psychology* 50, no. 5 (1986), 936–41.

[20] Drucker, *Management*, 435.

[21] John C. Maxwell, *Teamwork 101: What Every Leader Needs to Know* (Nashville: Thomas Nelson, 2009), 72.

[22] Pauline Graham, editor, *Mary Parker Follett: Prophet of Management, A Celebration of Writings from the 1920s* (Boston: Harvard Business School, 1995), 67–68.

[23] John Stott, *Christ in Conflict: Lessons from Jesus and His Controversies* (Downers Grove, IL: InterVarsity, 2013), 9.

[24] Welch, *Jack: Straight from the Gut*, 96.

[25] Sy Landau, Barbara Landau, and Daryl Landau, *From Conflict to Creativity: How Resolving Workplace Disagreements Can Inspire Innovation and Productivity* (San Francisco: Jossey-Bass, 2001), 163.

[26] Charlan Nemeth, *In Defense of Troublemakers: The Power of Dissent in Life and Business* (New York: Basic Books, 2018), 7–8.

[27] Landau, *From Conflict to Creativity*, 47.

[28] Francesca Gino, *Rebel Talent: Why It Pays to Break the Rules at Work and in Life* (New York: Dey St., 2018), 67.

[29] Richard Tanner Pascale, *Managing on the Edge: How the Smartest Companies Use Conflict to Stay Ahead* (New York: Touchstone, 1990), 254.

30 Steven R. Covey, "Habit 5: Seek First to Understand, Then to Be Understood," accessed April 29, 2021, https://www.franklincovey.com/the-7-habits/habit-5/.

31 Welch, *Jack: Straight from the Gut*, 104.

32 Nemeth, *In Defense of Troublemakers*, 116.

33 Lucius Annaeus Seneca, *On the Shortness of Life*, C. D. N. Costa, trans. (New York: Penguin, 2005), 1–2.

34 Lloyd John Ogilvie, *Quiet Moments with God: Prayers and Promises for Each New Day* (Eugene, OR: Harvest House, 1997), February 18.

35 Steven G. Rogelberg, *The Surprising Science of Meetings: How You Can Lead Your Team to Peak Performance* (New York: Oxford University Press, 2019), ix.

36 Leo Gough, *C. Northcote Parkinson's Parkinson's Law: A Modern-Day Interpretation of a Management Classic* (Oxford: Infinite Ideas, 2011), 8.

37 "Quotes by Amelia Earhart," accessed July 24, 2021, https://www.ameliaearhart.com/quotes/.

38 "Persistent," Cambridge dictionary, https://dictionary.cambridge.org/us/dictionary/english/persistent.

39 Quote Investigator, accessed July 24, 2021, https://quoteinvestigator.com/2013/08/21/effort/.

40 Tom Carter, ed., *2200 Quotations from the Writings of Charles H. Spurgeon* (Grand Rapids, MI: Baker, 1988), 167.

41 Billy Graham, "Sermon: The Rev. Billy Graham," Washington National Cathedral, September 14, 2001, https://cathedral.org/sermons/sermon-9/.

42 Charles Hanson Towne (1877–1949), "Around the Corner," public domain.

43 Glenn Van Ekeren, ed., *Speaker's Sourcebook II* (Englewood Cliffs, NJ: Prentice-Hall, 1994), 359.

44 Seneca, *On the Shortness of Life*, 4.

45 This story of a miraculous feast is told in all four Gospels; the version summarized here is from Mark 6:30–44.

[46] Nemeth, *In Defense of Troublemakers*, 12.

[47] Ibid., 106.

[48] Graham, *Mary Parker Follett*, 86.

[49] Gino, *Rebel Talent*, 91.

[50] Bryan Hancock, Elizabeth Hioe, and Bill Schaninger, "The Fairness Factor in Performance Management," *McKinsey Quarterly*, April 2018, https://www.mckinsey.com/business-functions/people-and-organizational-performance/our-insights/the-fairness-factor-in-performance-management.

[51] MacArthur, *Twelve Ordinary Men*, 4.

[52] Hancock, Hioe, and Schaninger, "The Fairness Factor in Performance Management," 5.

[53] Bailey, *Learning to Lead Like Jesus*, 177.

[54] Susan M. Heathfield, "Use Coaching to Improve Employee Performance," The Balance Careers, January 5, 2021, https:the balancecareers.com/use-coaching-to-improve-employee-performance-1918083.

[55] Bob Briner and Ray Pritchard, *The Leadership Lessons of Jesus: A Timeless Model for Today's Leaders* (Nashville, TN: B&H, 1998), 194–95, 198.

[56] Hancock, Hioe, and Schaninger, "The Fairness Factor," https://www.mckinsey.com/business-functions/people-and-organizational-performance/our-insights/the-fairness-factor-in-performance-management.

[57] Rosanne Lim, "Top 10 Main Causes of Project Failure," Project-Management.com, September 29, 2021, https://project-management.com/top-10-main-causes-of-project-failure/.

[58] Simon Swords, "Why Software Projects Fail & 6 Strategies to Make Them Succeed," Atlascode, February 4, 2020, https://www.atlascode.com/blog/why-software-projects-fail/#Percentage_of_Projects_That_Fail.

[59] James Anthony, "Ninety-Five Essential Project Management Statistics 2020/2021 Market Share and Data Analysis, Three Key Project Management Statistics You Should Know," The

State of Project Management Annual Report, 2019, Wellington, https://financesonline.com/35-essential-project-management-statistics-analysis-of-trends-data-and-market-share/.

60 Wellington Limited, *The State of Project Management 2021* (Windsor, Berkshire: Wellington Limited, 2021), 13.

61 Frank Sesno, *Ask More: The Power of Questions to Open Doors, Uncover Solutions, and Spark Change* (New York: Amacom, 2017), 1.

62 Derek Kidner, "Jerusalem Under Nehemiah" map, Ezra and Nehemiah: An Introduction and Commentary (Downers Grove, IL: InterVarsity, 1979), 95.

63 "Section," Merriam Webster Dictionary, https://www.merriam-webster.com/dictionary/section?utm_campaign=sd&utm_medium=serp&utm_source=jsonld.

64 Cyril J. Barber, *Nehemiah and the Dynamics of Effective Leadership* (Neptune, NJ: Loizeaux Brothers, 1999), 83.

65 "Quote by J. Willard Marriott," Breakthrough Quotes, accessed November 18, 2021, https://breakthroughquotes.com/quote/j-willard-marriott/its-the-little-things-that-make-the-big-things-possible-only-close-attention-to-the-fine-details-of-any-operation-makes-the-operation-first-class/.